The Gertrude Clarke Whittall
Poetry and Literature Fund

The Gertrude Clarke Whittall Poetry and Literature Fund was established in the Library of Congress in December 1950, through the generosity of Mrs. Gertrude Clarke Whittall, in order to create a center in this country for the development and encouragement of poetry, drama, and literature. Mrs. Whittall's earlier benefactions include the presentation to the Library of a number of important literary manuscripts, a gift of five magnificent Stradivari instruments, the endowment of an annual series of concerts of chamber music, and the formation of a collection of music manuscripts that has no parallel in the Western Hemisphere.

The Poetry and Literature Fund allows the Library to offer poetry readings, lectures, conferences, and dramatic performances. The proceedings of this conference are published by the Library to reach a wider audience and as a contribution to literary history and criticism.

Contents

Preface	vii
List of Conference Speakers	viii
Introduction	1
Nineteen Eighty-Four: The Text	3
Peter Davison, "What Orwell Really Wrote" 5	
Discussion 19	
George Orwell: The Man	23
Jenni Calder, "Orwell the Man" 25	
Peter Stansky, "The Englishness	
of George Orwell" 39	
Discussion 50	
Nineteen Eighty-Four: The Book	55
Denis Donoghue, *"Nineteen Eighty-Four:*	
Politics and Fable" 57	
Alfred Kazin, " 'Not One of Us':	
George Orwell and *Nineteen Eighty-Four"* 70	
Jeffrey Meyers, *"Nineteen Eighty-Four:*	
A Novel of the 1930s" 79	
Discussion 89	
Nineteen Eighty-Four: Its Meaning Today	95
Bernard Crick, "The Reception of	
Nineteen Eighty-Four" 97	
Nathan A. Scott, Jr., "Orwell's Legacy" 104	
Discussion 115	
Bibliography: A Selected List of References	121
Marguerite D. Bloxom	

Preface

An international roster of Orwell experts gathered at the Library of Congress on April 30 and May 1, 1984, for a conference chaired by the Library's consultant in poetry, Anthony Hecht, and sponsored by the Library's Gertrude Clarke Whittall Poetry and Literature Fund. The four sessions of the conference were: "What Orwell Really Wrote," "Orwell: The Man," "*Nineteen Eighty-Four*: The Book," and "*Nineteen Eighty-Four*: Its Meaning in 1984." After the formal papers in each session, some dialog with the audience was invited. This publication presents the full-length addresses (of which abbreviated versions were delivered at the conference) and summarizes the subsequent floor discussion.

The Library conceived of the two-day event as very much a unity, and most members of the audience were present for all the sessions. In some respects, it would have been more distinctive for the Library of Congress *not* to have an Orwell conference in 1984, since so many occurred elsewhere. However, without apology the Library believes that this is one that will be remembered. One example: in order to be present and lead off the conference, Peter Davison rearranged his schedule, which also included a speech less than twenty-four hours later at University College in London to open an Orwell exhibit there. In short, some people went to a great deal of trouble to take part in the conference, and we believe the rewards justified the effort.

John C. Broderick
Assistant Librarian for Research Services

The Conference Speakers

Jenni Calder, born in Chicago, now teaches in the Education Department of the Royal Scottish Museum in Edinburgh; and is the author of *Chronicles of Conscience: A Study of George Orwell and Arthur Koestler* and *Huxley and Orwell: Brave New World and Nineteen Eighty-Four*.

Bernard Crick, born in London, member of the Fabian Society and the Study of Parliament Group Reform Club, past professor of Political Theory and Institutions, University of Sheffield (England), is author of *The American Science of Politics*, among several political works, and of *George Orwell: A Life*.

Peter Davison is a professor at Darwin College, University of Canterbury, Kent, England; editor of *Nineteen Eighty-Four: The Facsimile* (over half of Orwell's working manuscript of the novel, with Mr. Davison's line-by-line guide to the author's revisions) and general editor of the projected seventeen-volume *George Orwell: The Complete Works*.

Denis Donoghue, born in Tullow, Ireland, is Henry James Professor of English at New York University and member of the board of the Abbey Theatre, Dublin; author of *The Integrity of Yeats, Jonathan Swift: A Critical Introduction, Sovereign Ghosts: Studies in Imagination*, and *Ferocious Alphabets*.

Anthony Hecht, chairman of the conference, winner of both Pulitzer and Bollingen Prizes in Poetry, has served the Library of Congress as consultant in poetry, 1982–84. Upon completion of his 1984 term at the Library, he returned to the University of Rochester, where he is John H. Deane Professor of Rhetoric and Poetry.

Alfred Kazin, Distinguished Professor of English at the City University of New York Graduate School and Hunter College, is author of *On Native Grounds, The Inmost Leaf, Starting Out in the Thirties, New York Jew*, and *American Procession*.

Jeffrey Meyers, born in New York City, has been professor of English at the University of Colorado at Boulder since 1975. His books include *A Reader's Guide to George Orwell* and *George Orwell: The Critical Heritage*.

Nathan Scott, Jr., taught for more than twenty years at the University of Chicago, where he was Shailer Mathews Professor of Theology and Literature. Since 1976 he has been at the University of Virginia, where he is William R. Kenan, Jr., Professor of Religious Studies and also professor of English. Among his numerous books are *Samuel Beckett*, *The Broken Center: Studies in the Theological Horizon of Modern Literature*, *Albert Camus*, *Negative Capability: Studies in the New Literature and the Religious Situation*, and *The Poetics of Belief*. He is a Fellow of the American Academy of Arts and Sciences.

Peter Stansky is Frances and Charles Field Professor of History at Stanford University; author of numerous studies of nineteenth- and twentieth-century English politics and political figures, in addition to *The Unknown Orwell* (with William Abrahams) and *On Nineteen Eighty-Four*.

Introduction

The Library of Congress has not been alone in noticing that this year has been made resonant by the title of a book of George Orwell's that appeared as long ago as 1949. Orwell's face has been featured on the cover of *Time*; Irving Howe edited a symposium on the book of the year, reviewed on the front pages of the *New York Times* by Arthur Schlesinger, Jr.; Walter Cronkite has furnished a preface to one of the multitude of new paperback editions; and virtually no one has failed to get into the act, either here or abroad. The *New York Times* for January 8 carried the following item:

A Soviet political journal claims in its current issue to have pinpointed the real-life version of George Orwell's novel, *1984*, in the United States under a Big Brother named Ronald Reagan. The weekly, *New Times*, published in Russian and in several foreign languages, including English, contends that all the characteristics of Orwell's nightmare society, including Newspeak, the Thought Police, and the Ministry of Truth, have their counterparts in modern America.

Victor Sopi, a writer for the Soviet publication, is said to have "summoned up Orwell's vision of society, in which the Thought Police watch citizens whether they are awake or asleep, in bath or in bed, and monitor friendships, families, even thoughts uttered in sleep. Doesn't that sound just like a directive of the FBI?" he asked. As if to confirm the Soviet vision, a classified ad appeared in the April issue of an American journal called *Boston Review*, and it reads as follows: "Big Brother for President. Join the 1984 Party. Full campaign packet includes button, party membership card, poster, and T-shirt (specify size). Send $10 to 1984 Party, P.O. Box 22545, Seattle, Washington."

If poor Eric Blair, the man whose pseudonym was George Orwell, had only lived to witness such fanfare and celebrity, he should probably have been wryly amused to find that his fiction has already been subjected to as much misconstruction as have some of Shakespeare's plays! It is in the hope of doing both honor and justice to the man and his work that this series of programs has been undertaken.

Anthony Hecht
Consultant in Poetry, 1982–84

Nineteen Eighty-Four:
The Text

What Orwell Really Wrote
by Peter Davison

I am greatly honored to address this gathering on "What Orwell *Really* Wrote." That catchpenny title conceals the hard fact that I am to talk about what is for most people *the* boring topic par excellence: analytical bibliography—textual analysis—and I am only too well aware of something Bruce Harkness once said: "Bibliographers are like socialists and Christians: walking arguments of the weakness of their cause."

I want to show you what has happened to the texts of George Orwell's nine books: what happened to several before they were printed, what happened in proof, and what happened in successive reprintings by different publishing houses. This is a result of going through publishers' files and some forty editions, line by line, comma by comma—including three editions in French. Theoretically, each English-language edition should read the same.

They don't. The differences are not few but to be numbered in hundreds—indeed, thousands. So, my task has been to try to restore what Orwell really wrote—or, more dangerously, intended to write—intended to have published. My task today is to try to explain and illustrate the nature of the problem and present some solutions.

The main burden of my talk will consider differences between editions, but to begin I shall speak briefly of deciding *what* Orwell wrote and *when*. I shall conclude by discussing some general implications. So, the traditional three parts: (1) What and When, (2) Restoring the Texts, (3) Problems and Critical Implications.

What and When?
There are few problems in trying to work out what Orwell wrote and when he wrote it. When and what he wrote at St. Cyprian's School and at Eton College present the most obvious difficulties.
(1) There is an undated letter home from St. Cyprian's school which begins:
Thanks for your letter. Today was a whole holiday, and we took our dinner out to East Dean, and went to have tea at Jevington. The tea was unspeakably horrible, though it did cost 1s. 6d.
This letter has been related to Orwell's first published poem, "Awake! Young Men of England" of 1914. In fact it must refer to his second poem of two

years later on the death of Lord Kitchener. The evidence consists of proximity to the end of term, amount of pocket money left over, whole-day holidays, and, not least, the incidence of mumps at St. Cyprian's. Comparison with the letters of Cyril Connolly—a schoolfriend of Orwell's—reveals not only that the fell hand of mumps was abroad, confirming the dating, but also tells, what we did not know—who sent the poem about Lord Kitchener to the Henley newspaper. It was neither the school nor Orwell's fond parents, but young Eric Blair himself. Incidentally, printed three columns to the left of Blair's/Orwell's poem is a rather revealing report entitled "The Problems of the Tramp." A glimpse into the future? That leads me to my second example.

(2) In Orwell's second year at Eton College he collaborated in the production of a handwritten journal called *Election Times*. One of the anonymous contributions is a dystopian story called "A Peep into the Future." Who wrote it? Of those involved, Denys King-Farlow thought it not by Orwell; Cyril Connolly and Sir Steven Runciman that it was his. There are two intriguing clues.

Clue 1: *Election Times* is entirely handwritten. "A Glimpse into the Future" is in Orwell's hand, but that is not conclusive evidence that the story is his, as he might have copied out someone else's work. However there is a telltale spelling mistake. The "mighty woman" of the story sticks out her chin "agressively"—with one *g*. That spelling is characteristic of Orwell from 1918 to *Nineteen Eighty-Four*, as I shall show you. Of course Orwell may have copied incorrectly what was writ correctly—we are not in the realms of absolute proof.

Clue 2: The protagonist of the story has a curious name: Pigling Hill. Jacintha Buddicom, a childhood friend of Orwell's, has recalled (without reference to this story, incidentally) that amongst young Blair's favorite books at this time were Wells's *Modern Utopia*—he told her "he might write that kind of book himself"—and Beatrix Potter's *Pigling Bland,* which she and Eric "adored." Eric read it over to her twice, from beginning to end, when she was ill, in order to cheer her up. Not proof, but intriguing conjunctions: Modern Utopia, Pigling, and one g for *aggressive.*

Let me now jump ahead, first to *Burmese Days* and then to *Nineteen Eighty-Four.*

(3) A number of preliminary sketches for *Burmese Days* have survived. Some are written on Government of Burma paper (which has printing stock dates) and some are watermarked. As so often, this is only of negative help, except for "The Autobiography of John Flory." The watermark of the paper on which this was typed was first recorded only in 1928. It is unlikely that the paper was available any earlier than 1927—when Orwell left Burma—and very unlikely that it was to be found in Burma by then. The story must have been typed (if not handwritten) after Orwell's return from Burma.

I cannot date the other sketches for *Burmese Days* in this way but I can offer an observation about one of them. It has been suggested that Flory's autobiography is written "in prison, awaiting execution" (Crick, 195). It is more probable, I think, that Flory is writing deep in the jungle where there will be no one "whose hand could form the letters" of his epitaph (as Flory puts it), suffering from excess of drink and women (as would have been Lackersteen's fate were not his wife with him on those jungle tours). Here the clue is the correct reading and interpretation of the place where Flory describes the events as taking place: not "Nyauglebiu" (not, I think, a Burmese place-name), but "Nyaunglebin," which means "The Four Banyan Trees," a not uncommon name for a jungle village in Burma.

(4) To conclude this section let me turn to the identification of a single page of the 183 which survive of Orwell's drafts for *Nineteen Eighty-Four*. This is a fair-typed page numbered 239. It is typed on one of Orwell's typewriters—a portable—and, surprise, surprise, that word *agressive* turns up with a single *g*. Everything pointed to Orwell having typed this page. But did he? I had doubts I could not quite formulate and the solution—for such it really is this time—might serve as a useful warning to those who (like me) are accustomed in Elizabethan textual studies to using type-face and spelling idiosyncrasies for the identification of compositors—revealing "who did the work."

It turned out that whilst Orwell was away in Jura he let his London flat to Mrs. Miranda Wood—then Mrs. Miranda Christen. In her second summer there, 1947, she was awaiting naturalization papers, being technically a German citizen, and also awaiting a passage back to Singapore by ship, both lengthy procedures in the aftermath of war. During the summer of 1947 she did some typing for Orwell. About every two weeks a batch of material would arrive through the mail and, using the portable typewriter she found in the flat, she made fair and carbon copies. These she then posted back to Orwell in Jura. The version sent to Mrs. Wood was, as she has described it in a private memoir she sent me, "presumably the initial draft." It was

> partly self-typed, partly handwritten. The writing was neat and legible with alterations and inserts carefully indicated and unfamiliar names and words spelled out meticulously. I was also provided with a separate glossary of Newspeak.

Nineteen Eighty-Four was not all that Mrs. Wood typed for Orwell: "One day there was a separate sheaf of papers in the package. It was a bleary typescript of the essay "Such, Such Were the Joys" to be re-done. It looked as if it had been lying around for a considerable time." So much for its being written about 1947.

The only page to survive of all those that Mrs. Wood typed is 239. She was able to identify that when examining the originals of this facsimile when they were in London in November 1983.

Now, Mrs. Wood, when typing Orwell's draft—on Orwell's own portable—repeated his misspelling, *agression*. Until I knew of Mrs. Wood's part in this story I had assumed, naturally enough, given the evidence of the typewriter and this idiosyncratic spelling, that page 239 must be Orwell's own typing. But the evidence proved misleading and the facts could only be established by external evidence of a kind that turned up fortuitously—evidence which no editor would dare invent to prove a theory.

Alas, that glossary of Newspeak has not survived.

This is not, perhaps, quite the context in which to expatiate on differences between the drafts of *Nineteen Eighty-Four* and the final version. But you might like to know of three passages omitted from the final version. Passages cut by Orwell include a horrific account of the lynching of a pregnant black woman and treatment of her aborted child: "The crowd played football with it"; a description, worked over several times, of Winston's arrival at O'Brien's flat; and a brief encounter after that meeting, when Julia and Winston had revealed to O'Brien their opposition to Big Brother's régime. The draft, as revised, has this rather touching passage:

He had gone perhaps two hundred metres, and was in the dark patch midway between two street lamps, when he was startled by something soft bumping against him. The next moment Julia's arms were clinging tightly round him.

"You see I've broken my first order," she whispered with her lips close against his ear. "But I couldn't help it. We hadn't fixed up about tomorrow. Listen." In the usual manner, she gave him instructions about their next meeting. "And now, good-night, my love, good-night!"

She kissed his cheek almost violently a number of times, then slipped away into the shadow of the wall and promptly disappeared. Her lips had been cold, and in the darkness it had seemed to him that her face was pale. He had a curious feeling that although the purpose for which she had waited was to arrange another meeting, the embrace she had given him was intended as some kind of good-bye.

Orwell objected strongly to the prepublication censorship which his work suffered but in the draft he himself toned down a passage. The published text tells how the Thought Police had "shown him photographs. Some of them were photographs of Julia and himself. Yes, even . . . ." The first draft is more specific explaining that "Some were of Julia and himself in the act of making love." Orwell himself toned that down.

Restoration

For this new edition almost forty earlier editions, several sets of proofs, and typescripts of *Animal Farm* and *Nineteen Eighty-Four* have been collated word for word, comma by comma. I do not deceive myself that I have spotted every difference. There is no more sleep-inducing task than collating.

I have also checked the French editions of *Down and Out in Paris and London* and *Homage to Catalonia* and richly rewarding that proved—even though the French translation of *Homage to Catalonia* was not published until five years after Orwell's death. The generosity of its translator, Madame Yvonne Davet, has enabled me to obtain for publication seventeen letters by George Orwell going back to before the 1939–45 war; to learn, what I think was not known, that several of his books had been translated into French before that war, including *Homage to Catalonia*; to recover a reading; and to learn of the title he would have preferred for the French edition of *Animal Farm:* "Union des républiques socialistes animales"—URSA—the Bear.

A letter from Eileen Blair produced another reading. Orwell records in *The Road to Wigan Pier,* "For the first time in my life, in a bare patch beside the line, I saw rooks treading." We can tell from the proof that what was originally set was *courting*—but that was too risqué a word in those days (hence the fun in Wilfred Pickles's question in a popular radio show of a few years on: "Are ye coortin'?"). But Eileen's letter of January 17, 1937, says that what Orwell had originally written was *copulating*—as in the *Diary.*

A postcard found in the files of Allen & Unwin recorded the initiation of Orwell's revision of racial names. In a passage in his article "As I please" for December 10, 1943, he recorded that he was revising his proofs and changing names resented by people of the races to which they referred—*Chinese* for *Chinaman,* *Moslem* for *Mohamedan.* "Even the Left Wing Press . . . did not bother to find out which names were resented by other races." *Negro,* he said, should always have a capital *N*—times have changed even more, of course, but in his day, Orwell was clearly in the van of change. In Allen & Unwin's file is a card dated June 21, 1943, about the BBC talks which Orwell was preparing for publication. One of the speakers, Cedric Dover, specifically asked that a capital always be given to the word *Negro.* Thus, the 1947 proof of *Coming Up for Air* records just such a change. But should not an editor retroactively make such changes to earlier texts? Would that not be what his author would require?—would now intend?

But of all the resources apart from the texts themselves available to an editor of Orwell's books, the richest haul is that located in the Gollancz files. Through the generosity of Livia Gollancz, Ian Angus and I were able with her guidance to unearth details of much that had been omitted as a result of in-house censorship in the 1930s. This affects several books but I shall stick to two for which the scale and nature of change must affect our interpretation of the novels: *Keep the Aspidistra Flying* and *A Clergyman's Daughter.* This correspondence suggests, incidentally, that the part played by Norman Collins in requiring changes has been considerably exaggerated, resented though it was by Orwell. Hardly at all for *Burmese Days;* belatedly for *Keep the Aspidistra Flying.*

I ought, however briefly, to reiterate what I have written elsewhere, that that in-house censorship, however absurd it may seem to us, was thoroughly understandable looked at from a vulnerable publisher's point of view in the 1930s. It is worth remembering that, quite apart from libel actions, which such a publisher could ill afford to engage in, Gollancz in the mid-thirties was closer in time to Henry Vizetelly, condemned to a year's prison for publishing Zola, than we are to the events I am describing.

The chief anxiety provoked by *Keep the Aspidistra Flying* was the use of real advertising slogans. "Have a Camel" had to be omitted; "Earn £5 in Your Free Time" had to be omitted; so had "Are you a Highbrow . . . Dandruff is the Reason"—it was replaced by "Kiddies Clamour for their Breakfast Crisps." A "Night Starvation" advertisement replaced "Prompt Relief for Feeble Kidneys" and "Guiness is Good for you" was cut out and replaced by "Get that waistline back to normal"—and so on.

That revolting advertising character, "Corner Table," was a substitution for a real advertising character, "Roland Butta," who had appeared in the original text. Notice, the same number of letters are used. What particularly incensed Orwell was that many of the changes were not made until late—until the proof stage—when he was in Wigan—and he had to provide replacements of similar length. That also meant that links he had built into the story were lost. Thus, Orwell had called the claims of medical advertisements "garbage": a few pages away he described the work of the popular novelists Warwick Deeping and Ethel M. Dell as "garbage." In a letter to Leonard Moore, his literary agent (an extract of which was sent to Collins, who passed it to Gollancz), Orwell complained bitterly of changes required at proof stage. He would, he wrote, "have entirely rewritten the first chapter and modified several others . . . . In general a passage of prose or even a whole chapter revolves round one or two key phrases, and to remove these, as was done in this case, knocks the whole thing to pieces." I suspect that one of the things Orwell had in mind was the omission of "garbage" to describe the work of "the Deepings and Dells," so linking it with the garbage of advertising claims for miracle cures.

One particular reading that has been recovered might be of interest: Gordon Comstock (and if the name *Gordon* glanced at Orwell's dislike of the Scotch at this period of his life, may not *Comstock* also have a specific significance? Gollancz's lawyer was to ask whether this, as other names, was of a real person. Orwell could readily say it wasn't—but had he in mind, given his experience of censorship, the founder of the New York Society for the Suppression of Vice, Anthony Comstock, instigator of the "Comstock Act" of 1873?). Gordon Comstock is described as "sucking the soothing smoke" of a cheap Player's Weight cigarette in the novel as published. The Gollancz files show that originally Orwell wrote "sucking the papery smoke." The libel lawyer was unsure of the meaning of *papery* here but thought it likely to be actionable and required it to be changed. Orwell changed it to *acrid*—but that would not do either and so we have the quite different meaning, soothing smoke. Incidentally, *papery*, Orwell explained, implied that one tasted more cigarette paper than tobacco.

Study of these files enables a fair amount of the original text to be recovered. Often we can only indicate where changes are to be made. This is particularly significant in *Keep the Aspidistra Flying* in the matter of Gordon's abortive love-making with Rosemary in the woods at Burnham Beeches. The lawyer's advice to Gollancz was that these pages should "be considered very carefully from the point of view of alleged obscenity." Orwell's reply is poignant: "I have altered certain passages here in Mr. Gollancz's office and I think he has now no objection." Gollancz walked a knife-edge in the matter of censorship and I think his caution justified; he was encouraging a new author. But one cannot help but see Orwell, however much it was unintended by Gollancz, as rewriting his essay—his letters home as it were—in the headmaster's study, on less disturbing lines.

If a fair amount can be restored to *Keep the Aspidistra Flying*, the same cannot be said for *A Clergyman's Daughter*, although the changes required are even more far-reaching. Some specific changes can be made. "Rushington" is "Carshalton"; the public library is specified as that at Lambeth; it was not merely the *local* bank manager who squandered money on a bigamous marriage but *Barclay's* bank manager. These changes were part of a policy of delocalizing the novel—the same policy that had been adopted by Gollancz for the English edition of *Burmese Days* in the preceding year. There was also caution in referring to the *Church Times* and *High Churchman's Gazette* just as the name of the newspaper was changed in *Burmese Days* and for *Keep the Aspidistra Flying* the name of the biweekly local paper that reported Gordon's drunken brawl was suppressed—*The Hampstead and Camden Town Messenger*. Thus, Victor Stone, the church schoolmaster, is put "in the forefront of every assault upon Modernists and atheists," whereas Orwell originally wrote (and I have restored), "especially when the Church Times was at its chosen sport of baiting Modernists and atheists."

Now here, in both novels, we can restore what Orwell originally wrote. What is not possible is to restore passages which have been extensively modified but for which all we have is a general indication—and there are some thirty of these in *A Clergyman's Daughter,* some spanning several pages at a time. It was probably the prospective parliamentary candidate Blifil-Gordon who was once described as a "Roman Catholic Jew," but that description was removed as being too like someone then in the House of Commons. But I cannot restore the actual text. Dorothy's interview with Mrs. Creevy was toned down "with a view to making Mrs. Creevy out a somewhat less barefaced swindler"; "The description of Dorothy's first lesson at the school has been toned down, with a view to giving a less exaggerated impression of the low standard prevailing in these schools"—and I am quoting Orwell's own words: "General remarks on private schools toned down slightly and put in a perhaps more plausible manner"; "I have greatly toned down this conversation" (in which Mrs. Creevy rebukes Dorothy for her teaching methods). And no less than three times references had to be cut from the novel which said that if Dorothy lost her job at Mrs. Creevy's school, "she would be on the streets again."

However, perhaps the most significant omission of all, given the puzzling development in which Dorothy seems to lose her memory, is a reference early on in the novel that Mr. Warburton had "tried to rape" Dorothy. I guess that this cut was replaced by the reference to Warburton "making love to her, violently, outrageously, even brutally." Presumably there was once a placing here, and perhaps elsewhere, that Dorothy was the victim of rape. Unfortunately for Orwell, just as in his attempts to represent real-life advertising slogans, it was too dangerous to permit reality to break in. He was not allowed to say Dorothy was raped. That not only has, for *A Clergyman's Daughter,* a damaging effect on the novel's narrative line, but, more generally, blurs that delicate relationship between the factual and the creative, the documentary and the fictional, which he was exploring and which, I believe, he developed in so interesting and valuable a manner.

It was never intended that when these nine books were reprinted that I should provide footnotes. A General Introduction to the nine volumes, yes; a textual note with a few selected readings for each book (and I have adopted the scheme devised by the late T.J.B. Spencer for the New Penguin Shakespeare), yes. But then, as I shall explain in a moment, new material emanating from Orwell was found in footnotes added to the French editions of *Down and Out* and *Homage to Catalonia,* and those, I thought, should be added to the new English editions. There are already authorial footnotes in those books and a few more, originating from Orwell, would strike a reader as perfectly natural. But what of *A Clergyman's Daughter*? Not to provide some sort of commentary relevant to the passages "toned down," to use Orwell's own repeated phrase, would continue to ensure that less than justice was done to *A Clergyman's Daughter.*

If one could note, in Orwell's own words, how the book had had to be modified, a better impression might be given of his achievement and, perhaps, readers would more readily understand why this novel and *Keep the Aspidistra Flying,* garbled in this enforced rewriting, sometimes even rewriting done in the publisher's office, came to be rejected by their author and thought not worth reprinting. Thus, this new edition, as well as making the textual modifications for which there is clear evidence, will note, in Orwell's own words, where the novel was garbled to suit the "censor."

Before I move on to consider the revision of *Homage to Catalonia,* let me mention one last restoration of many that could be selected. This applies only to English editions of *Nineteen Eighty-Four,* so far as I am aware. At the end of the novel, as the typescript and editions published in Orwell's lifetime indisputably show—and as American editions show—Winston Smith succumbed and admitted that $2 + 2 = 5$. The English hard-back editions lost the 5 from 1951 onwards and the Penguin paperback editions followed suit. Even the special reprintings for 1984—by Secker's *and* Penguin—lack the 5. I know of no evidence to suggest that Orwell changed his mind. Such hope as there was lay with the proles, not with would-be intellectuals such as Winston, as Orwell was at pains to point out—and hence, of course, his own toning down of the proles' reactions to the newsreel scenes of violence. All that happened, I think, was that in 1951 a figure dropped out of the printing forme and, in consequence, the meaning of the novel was inverted.

I should now like to turn to an aspect of editing these nine books that takes the editor beyond what might, conventionally, be thought of as the limits of the editorial task; i.e., to the modification and expansion of a text.

The books in question are *Down and Out in Paris and London* and *Homage to Catalonia*; both involve the French translations (of 1935 and 1955 respectively) and for *Homage to Catalonia* there are also Orwell's instructions to his literary executors—a properly witnessed, signed, and dated document.

Comparison of the English and French texts of both books shows that not only are many of the indications for swear-words filled in (in French, of course) but that there are additional footnotes. These notes seem to have two sources: those contributed by the translators to explain the text to their readers and those which must derive from Orwell. There is a short disquisition on the Hindi equivalents of the French *tu* and *vous*; and an account of the derivation of the English slang *barnshoot* and its origin in the Hindi, *bahinchut*, and what that word means. There is in *Homage to Catalonia* a marvelous explanation for the letters DSO—properly a military decoration, the Distinguished Service Order. The text reads, "Thomas Parker got a bullet through the top of his thigh, which, as he said, was nearer to being a DSO than he cared about." I doubt if most contemporary English readers—never mind French readers in 1955—understood what DSO meant here. And I doubt if the translator knew. The explanation given in a footnote in the French edition must, surely, derive from Orwell: wounded in the top of the thigh, Thomas Parker came near to suffering his "Dickie Shot Off"—D.S.O. I have added that footnote.

I have tried to distinguish between what might stem from Orwell and what from the translators and have added as footnotes, translated into English, those that might be Orwell's and as end-notes those that might be the translators'.

As for swear-words—the crucial advice to an editor for the 1984 edition is to be found in *La Vache Enragée*, the 1935 French version of *Down and Out*:

> Ce mot et les mots en italique qui suivent sont figurés par des tirets dans l'édition anglaise; nous les rétablissons ici en toutes lettres d'après les indications de l'auteur.

In brief: where the English is content with dots and dashes, the French has restored the full word in the light of the author's indications. No wonder Orwell so approved of the French translation! Thus, in the English edition of *Homage to Catalonia*, we find "B——— the telescope! Benjamin's waiting outside." In the French edition, preferring end-rhyme to alliteration we find "Je m'en fous de la long-vue." Well, I have restored *Bugger*—upon which word Orwell has a disquisition in a footnote to the French edition of *Down and Out*—also recovered and restored.

But I have gone farther. As Orwell asked that the Spanish used in the English edition of *Homage to Catalonia* should be corrected, and as he so admired the French translation of *Down and Out*, I have corrected the idiomatic French so that it accords with the French edition, *La Vache Enragée* of

1935. Thus, menu terms are corrected and one has, for example, *Range-toi* for *Sauve-toi*. All this is, of course, recorded in the Textual Notes. (The new French translation, *Dans la Dèche* (1982), is more conservative. It does modify some of the French and cuts most of the footnotes added in 1935— though the rationale for that is obscure.)

But *Homage to Catalonia* presents a much more difficult problem, involving for its solution the participation of the editor, in however slight a way, in the writing of the book as revised. Orwell left instructions for changes. These I have carried out. Some, such as relegating chapters 5 and 11 to appendixes, were also required of that 1955 French translation, but some are peculiar to this new edition. Inevitably there are consequential changes in moving two chapters from the middle of a book to its end—what is said to have been written about in the last chapter becomes "as will be written about in Appendix I," say. What leads to editorial complications is the confusion in the minds of Orwell and many historians as to who attacked the Telephone Exchange in Barcelona. Orwell thought it was the Civil Guards, and although Geoffrey Gorer wrote to him on April 18, 1938, to say he was wrong, it was only some time later that Orwell realized he had been mistaken. He therefore required that wherever "Civil Guards" stood in the text, it should be replaced by "Assault Guards." But in practice, this is not always easy and no such changes are made in the 1955 French translation. Take this sentence: "It was easy to dodge the Assault Guard patrols; the danger was the Civil Guards in the 'Moka.' " Make the switch and that would become: "It was easy to dodge the Assault Guard patrols; the danger was the Assault Guards." In addition, Orwell also required that the fact that the Civil Guards were hated should be specifically mentioned—but they have been excised. I hope I have resolved these problems in an unobtrusive manner in the spirit of the author's wishes. But it does mean an editorial contribution to the text, however modest.

The final aspect of restoration to which I wish to refer is illustrative matter. The first English and American editions of *The Road to Wigan Pier* included thirty-two pages of plates. They have never been included in later editions and this is, I think, a great pity, not only because the book is impoverished without them but because they are at the beginning of a documentary tradition (in accord with the British film documentaries of that time, such as *Housing Conditions*, 1935) that is perhaps best-known in the juxtaposition of text and illustration in England in *Picture Post* and in America in *Let Us Now Praise Famous Men*.

But who suggested these illustrations for *The Road to Wigan Pier* and where did they come from? In going through the Gollancz files with Miss Gollancz I was fortunate to come across not only letters seeking illustrations but also the name of the person who suggested those names and, quite remarkably, the scrap of blotting paper upon which Victor Gollancz had jotted down the names of potential suppliers of photographs. It was possible to relate the names on the blotting paper to the surviving copy letters asking for photographs and some of the replies. It is certain that Orwell met Gollancz in his office on

Monday, December 21, 1936, just before he left to fight in Spain, two days later. They presumably discussed illustrations because on December 22, Norman Collins, deputy chairman of Gollancz, wrote to various people to say that their names had been suggested—and suggested by Clough Williams Ellis, the architect and creator of the fantasy village of Portmeirion in Wales—a world away from the slums illustrated in *The Road to Wigan Pier.* Whether the initial idea was Orwell's, Ellis's, or Gollancz's I have not been able to ascertain. It was obviously a last-minute idea, for the book was published on March 8, 1937, a mere ten weeks after the photographs for illustrations were first requested. Orwell was in Spain and could not have seen any of them in advance. Incidentally, it was originally proposed to have forty-eight pages of plates, not thirty-two. The same text/picture technique was used eight months later for Wal Hannington's *The Distressed Areas.*

The last item under the heading *Restoration* is, to be frank, a cheat, for it was never intended to be published and so is an addition, not a restoration. I refer to Orwell's sketch of the village of Kyauktada in *Burmese Days*—a sketch which will be included as a frontispiece to the new edition.

As is well known, *Burmese Days* was first published in the United States. Gollancz had far from groundless anxieties about the danger of legal action were it to be published in England, but early in 1935 he asked Orwell to meet him and a lawyer to discuss changes. That meeting took place on February 22, 1935. It is worth noting Orwell's response to that meeting, especially in the light of his unhappiness at changes made in this and other novels. This is from his letter to Leonard Moore, his agent, on that very day:

> I saw Gollancz and his solicitor [no reference to Norman Collins] this afternoon and we had a long talk, and you will be glad to hear that they are quite ready to publish BURMESE DAYS, subject to a few trifling alterations which will not take more than a week.

Subject to a few trifling alterations! So much for garbling!

Just three weeks earlier, John R. Hall, book editor of the Democrat-News Printing Company, Missouri, had written to Orwell to say how much he had enjoyed *Burmese Days.* On the back of the letter is a sketch map drawn by Orwell. It would seem that the letter arrived opportunely and Orwell took it along to the meeting with Gollancz and the solicitor to show how much the book was appreciated in America—though that must be a guess. The map looks as if it were drawn by Orwell as part of the scheme for the delocalizing of the village where the action of *Burmese Days* takes place—delocalizing again, note. At its top is a list giving page numbers for topographical changes and other modifications, all of which I have been able to identify with changes made for the Gollancz, 1935 edition—changes sent to Gollancz six days later.

Problems and Critical Implications

Some of the problems and critical implications will already be apparent: to what extent should a foreign version be translated back to supplement the original English text? To what extent should an editor involve himself in the writing of an edition to meet his author's wishes? It will, I think, be realized that simply to reprint early editions would not wash; indeed, as Orwell revised in proof, it is not even wholly satisfactory to reprint his own typescripts where they survive, though I have restored his punctuation for *Animal Farm* and *Nineteen Eighty-Four* and various other presentational characteristics. Thus, instead of regularizing the capitalization of the "Seven Commandments," in *Animal Farm*, as, understandably, the subeditor did in 1945, I have retained lower-case initial letters when the words are first used—as Orwell does—and then used capitals, as Orwell does, when the Commandments become sacrosanct. Similarly the use of initial capitals for *War*, *Home*, and *Canal* have a particular implication in *Burmese Days*, unrecognized though this was in some of the earlier editions.

But when it comes to taking note of what Orwell proofread, especially what he proofread for a final edition in his lifetime, we are in difficulties. Thus, when Secker & Warburg reprinted *Coming Up for Air* in 1948, they adapted the Gollancz house style to theirs. Orwell read the proofs and presumably accepted the changes. On October 22, 1947, having checked those proofs, he proudly wrote to Roger Senhouse, one of Secker's directors, to say that he'd written the whole book without a single semicolon in it as he'd decided the semicolon was an unnecessary device. But if you look at that Secker edition you will find three semicolons have been added (quite sensibly). Either Orwell did not notice when he read the proofs or he did and the printer ignored his instructions. I suspect Orwell did not notice, otherwise he would hardly have written to Senhouse as he did.

The English and American editions of *Nineteen Eighty-Four* were prepared separately and simultaneously for the press. The American proofs were received after the English proofs and by then Orwell was so ill that he had arranged that Sir Richard Rees would read them through were he unable to do so. There are hundreds of differences between the two editions—hundreds. Most are in punctuation or stylistic. Thus, except in one instance, the American edition always changes the English *towards* to *toward*. But there are a number of verbal changes. What does an editor do? Orwell *did* read the American proofs after the English proofs. Do we assume he wanted changes from the English edition published a few weeks earlier? Thus in the English edition Orwell refers to one character's "thick negroid" lips; however, the American edition has "protuberant." A social change or authorial? Although most verbal and probably all punctuational changes are designed for American readers, in eleven instances I have accepted American readings as authorial revisions, ignoring hundreds of changes in accidentals and many verbal changes. But it will be apparent upon what a razor's edge is editorial decision-making here. Let me give you one instance of a change I have adopted from the American edition. The first English edition and typescript have:

Tillotson was busy on the same job as himself. There was no way of

knowing whose job would finally be accepted . . . .
The repeated *job* is very awkward and the American edition replaces the second *job* with *version*. But who can be sure? Changing punctuation is not peculiar to the American edition of *Nineteen Eighty-Four*. There are well over two hundred changes in the less than one hundred pages of the English edition of *Animal Farm*, so this editorial interference occurred on both sides of the Atlantic. Undoubtedly it has affected the rhetoric of these novels.

Orwell expressed to Roger Senhouse his belief that *on* and *to* should on occasion form one word, despite Senhouse's "archaic horror" of this form. On March 2, 1949, Orwell wrote from his hospital bed:

As to 'onto'. I know this is an ugly word, but I consider it to be necessary in certain contexts. If you say 'the cat jumped on the table' you may mean that the cat, already on the table, jumped up and down there. On the other hand, 'on to' (two words) means something different, as in 'we stopped at Barnet and then drove on to Hatfield'. In some contexts, therefore, one needs 'onto'. Fowler, if I remember correctly, doesn't altogether condemn it.

It will at once be apparent that Orwell might have made his rule rather clearer had he included an *onto* example, but his wishes are plain enough. Senhouse, archaic horror or no, did what Orwell wished, though he was to some extent circumvented by a combination of compositors and proofreaders. An editor is posed with some awkward problems if he is to realize Orwell's intentions. Certainly it is possible to "correct" instances where what appears in Orwell's typescript is not followed. Unfortunately, the distinction between *on to* and *onto* is not always quite so clear as Orwell implied and quite often he broke his own "rule." Does the editor correct Orwell? And for earlier volumes, do we argue that as Orwell passed the proofs of such books, or himself failed to distinguish correctly between the two forms, the "error" should be allowed to stand? Or would, as I suspect, Orwell, had he been alive to be asked, prefer an error to be corrected?

This little instance epitomizes a problem that pervades the editing of these nine books. *Coming Up for Air* presents a number of examples where *onto* appears in the Gollancz 1939 edition but is changed to *on to* in the 1948 Secker & Warburg edition (for which Orwell saw proofs). But that 1939 edition also gets Orwell's own rule wrong: "I chucked my hat on to the grass" (p. 109, 1. 4). On the assumption that, had this been pointed out to Orwell, he would have preferred *onto*, I have given that reading in the new edition. It is, of course, a dangerous assumption and one that can be much misused. Should one correct Orwell's arithmetic in *The Road to Wigan Pier*? One can see from Orwell's notes that he has in one instance got his sums wrong—divided two men's earnings incorrectly—so that the average pay after stoppages should be £2.10.6½ (*not* £2.11.4)—a reduction of 4/7½ (not 3/10).

I want to conclude with two editorial problems associated with *Burmese Days*. Orwell specifically rejected the Gollancz edition as garbled and, in his notes for his literary executors, said that that edition must not be followed.

Later editions—such as the Penguin of 1944—reverted, more or less, to the American first edition. Despite his letter to Moore, which described the changes as "trifling," they obviously rankled. But were *all* the changes then made solely on the grounds of in-house censorship? I think not—and there is a revealing clue that this "garbled" edition also contains authorially inspired revisions.

Among his instructions to his literary executors is one that requires that *sat* should be changed to *knelt* in the church scene at the very end of the novel. If you look at that rejected, garbled, Gollancz edition, you will find that Orwell had, in fact, already made the change to *knelt* in the course of meeting the solicitor's requirements for the publication of the "garbled" Gollancz edition. So it was not all garbled; and if there is one correct reading that Orwell can be shown to have forgotten, might there not be others? I have, I hope correctly, isolated a half-dozen more authorial revisions from that rejected Gollancz edition. Again, a dangerous, razor-edge practice.

I have left until last what must seem a particularly trivial matter: italicization. Trivial though it may seem, it can have significant implications for understanding—for literary criticism.

Burmese Days makes much use of "foreign" languages, which raises the question, "Foreign to whom?" Orwell castigates the English women who will not learn the language of the people among whom they are living. Flory, for all his faults, can speak Burmese and Hindi (as could Orwell, who also spoke Shaw-Karen as well as several European languages). Now, how are non-English words to be represented? When Flory speaks in native languages, he must, in the main, be rendered in English so the reader can know what is being said. Somehow, however, Orwell must get across the fact that there is a language divide.

The first American edition made very little use of italic and occasionally thought a foreign word a misprint for a more familiar English word—printing *piece* for *pice*, for example. Increasingly thereafter Gollancz, Penguin and Secker italicized and Orwell read the proofs of such editions. But italicization was not systematic. Thus *weiksa*, the Burmese word for *conjuror*, appears in the latest edition three times, once in italics, once in roman, and once in roman in single quotes. Furthermore, there is disagreement among the standard authorities as to which words have been assimilated into English and which are still alien. The *OED* regards *sahib* as alien but *syce*—a "groom"—as naturalized, which is sociologically interesting if nothing else.

I have tried to be rational without being rigid in these matters so far as the presentation of all nine books is concerned, but that still leaves a difficult problem to be resolved for italicization in *Burmese Days*. Clearly regularization was desirable and clearly words totally unfamiliar to a non-Burmese speaker should be italicized: thus *weiksa*, at each of its three appearances, should be italicized. Some words might reasonably be regarded as understood and could be left in roman: bazaar, chit, havildar, sahib (but not *sahiblog*), salaam, sepoy, and topi.

One word that appears time after time in its principal or derivative forms is *shiko*; its too-frequent italicization might well become a distraction, and it was decided to leave it in roman given that it became, for the purposes of this novel, a naturalized word. However, almost fifty words have been italicized at every appearance. One or two will be known to some English readers (*maidan* and *mali*, for example), but most will be unfamiliar. The result is a considerable increase in italicization, though not, I hope, to the point of affectation or pedantry. One effect will be, I think, that Orwell's story will be presented in a way he would wish: it is the British who are aliens in this society and the language in which the story must be told—English—is itself alien to the host people. From so simple a matter as which words are italicized, I hope a main thrust of Orwell's story will be made clearer to the reader. If we are to see our author, and not we ourselves, even such seeming trivia are significant.

I have done my best to present Orwell's work as I believe he would wish it to be presented, but it would be arrogant folly to pretend that I can please everyone with the decisions I have taken and in the preparation, printing, and proofreading of these nine books, errors must have crept in. In preparing this edition the nature of the task has, I believe, demanded that the editor go beyond what is customarily regarded as the editorial limit as contemporary scholarly editing is understood. I have had to recreate, so far as that is practicable, what Orwell originally intended to have published, and at times I have had to create a text not precisely formulated by the author. In so doing an editor walks a razor's edge, ever in danger of mistaking his own inclinations for his author's intentions. However, not to accept such a challenge, to shun the risks and play for safety, would, I believe, lead to an abrogation of the editorial task so far as the works of George Orwell are concerned.

If I have succeeded in anything it is, I hope, in making clear in my "General Introduction" that, despite all the care taken by everyone involved in the production of this edition, it should not be called *definitive*—a term I abhor. So, too, did Winston Smith, and, I guess, George Orwell. In a task of this kind, to claim definitiveness cannot but be *hybris*, and, rightly, that invites disaster. Ampleforth, you will recall, "was engaged in producing garbled versions—definitive texts they were called," said Winston Smith: the shadow of Editor Ampleforth has loomed large over me in my part of this enterprise.

Discussion

The opening question from the floor was what, in addition to Orwell's nine books, will constitute *The Complete Works of George Orwell* (in progress at the time of this conference). Mr. DAVISON replied, "absolutely everything," and gave several details: parts of letters that had been shortened or censored, the early stories, the diary and notes for *The Road to Wigan Pier*, the texts of plays, "everything he did, in fact." He and the publishers think it will be the first time a major twentieth-century author, who has a fairly large body of work, will be published absolutely in toto by modern scholarly methods. He went on to illustrate the interesting result of "breaking up the diaries with the letters and other items that were published at that time" with the example of the emendations to the manuscript of *The Road to Wigan Pier*: in juxtaposition in the forthcoming edition are the synchronous angry letter from Orwell to his agent, Leonard Moore, protesting the changes requested by his publisher, Gollancz; his letter to Gollancz with the changes; then his diary record of "that killing visit down Crippen's mine."

The matter of changes requested by the publisher was discussed at some length. Had Orwell insisted his book be published as written, the book, Mr. DAVISON answered, would have been withdrawn. The caution, not only of the publishers in England but also of the printers, was to avert lawsuits for obscenity, defamation, and libel. Therefore, if Orwell wanted his books published in England, "they had to be emasculated." In his view, Orwell must have realized that *A Clergyman's Daughter* was fragmented by the editorial changes. JEFFREY MEYERS asked whether the in-house censorship ever improved Orwell's work, and Mr. DAVISON answered that Harold Rubinstein, the lawyer for the Gollancz firm, who was also a sensitive literary critic and a playwright, would comment usefully from time to time upon stylistic and structural problems. Nonetheless, passages toned down because they might be libelous always weakened, delocalized, and worsened the book. In sum, Mr. DAVISON concluded, "I think it isn't a question here of the kind of literary editor who is giving advice as to how you might improve the novel; it's simply a matter of getting it through, so that it doesn't attract the attention of the law courts. . . . But that mustn't hide the fact that Harold Rubinstein was . . . quite well aware of the problems of the author."

Orwell had also to fight against the idea that the "house style" is sacrosanct. Comparing the Gollancz with the Secker and Warburg texts, Mr. DAVISON said that Secker and Warburg "got their comma pot out and [peppered] commas all over the place," but that, although Mr. DAVISON cannot prove it, the Gollancz texts probably represent what Orwell wrote, "because Gollancz couldn't afford copy-editors."

Mr. CRICK asked what will happen to the corrupt texts, the "Orwell that ordinary people read," after publication of the high-priced true texts that Mr. Davison's scholarly labors will provide; and whether a new copyright will protect Mr. Davison's labors after the year 2000. Mr. DAVISON believes there will be different copyright for some of the books, there being only one book that is not significantly different in the new edition (*Coming Up for Air*, with about forty changes), but said the copyright business is difficult. In answer to Mr. Crick's first question, the "fairly clear and fairly well sorted out" principle will be that the deluxe edition will bear the costs for producing the trade edition, in which Orwell's nine books should be out within the year. He does not know how long it will take for the eight volumes of Orwell's essays to appear in a trade edition.

In answer to a question from the floor about Orwell's choice of the title *Nineteen Eighty-Four*, Mr. DAVISON recalled that Orwell said in a letter: "I'm not sure whether to call the book 'The Last Man in Europe' or 'Nineteen Eighty-Four.' " In the beginning, the summer that he wrote the first fifty pages, Orwell was thinking of some thirty or so years ahead, a year that seemed to be a generation ahead, when his son would be thirty or thirty-five years old, and picked the date 1980. The following summer he wrote a full draft, and the summer after that—"by that stage, it's 1982"—he revised the whole draft. The reversal of dates, 1948/1984, for Orwell "had a certain irony, if nothing else . . . but that certainly wasn't the original conception."

Asked if Orwell's works had to be changed on grounds of political interference and compromise, Mr. DAVISON answered that, although he had difficulty getting *Homage to Catalonia* and *Animal Farm* printed, "the point was, they were printed in the form that he wished to have them printed. . . . No, I don't think they were ever changed on the grounds of political interference."

In a brief discussion about whether or not Orwell's thanking Victor Gollancz for writing the preface of *The Road to Wigan Pier* was ironic, Mr. DAVISON said he did not know, but thought not.

George Orwell: The Man

Orwell: The Man
by Jenni Calder

All writers are vain, selfish and lazy, and at the very bottom of their motives there lies a mystery. Writing a book is a horrible, exhausting struggle, like a long bout of some painful illness. One would never undertake such a thing if one were not driven on by some demon whom one can neither resist nor understand. For all one knows that demon is simply the same instinct that makes a baby squall for attention. And yet it is also true that one can write nothing reasonable unless one constantly struggles to efface one's own personality.

George Orwell, "Why I Write"

The first thing that needs to be said about Orwell the man is that he was a writer. This may seem to be stating the obvious, but we must remember that the most important thing about George Orwell, or Eric Blair, was that he wrote. The second is that the writing shaped the man as much as the man shaped the writing. The third is that although Eric Blair himself, by becoming George Orwell, by discouraging a biography, by talking about the need to efface personality, invites a separation between Eric Blair and George Orwell, between man and writer, no such separation is possible.

If we were to begin with the assumption that behind *Nineteen Eighty-Four*, *Animal Farm*, *Homage to Catalonia*, the early novels, the journalism, the documentary, the essays there is a deeply private person who is Eric Blair, then I think it unlikely that it would take us very far. I want to argue that the need to write, and the convictions that powered his writing, were an integral, probably the most radical—in the literal sense—part of Orwell's personality. Everything else that one might wish to say about him as a man is in some way absorbed or directed by his need to write and his enactment of that need.

The passage from "Why I Write," the essay published in 1946 that is so often used as a key to Orwell, is revealing, but it reveals contradictions rather than certainties. "All writers are vain, selfish and lazy." Why does Orwell say that? Writers are vain because they want to express themselves, they want to be read and taken notice of, they want to make an impression. They are selfish because writing, certainly if it is regarded as an art, is considered a rather special activity, and writers, like other artists, are considered rather special people for whom allowances have to be made. We know that there were times when Orwell regarded himself as exempt from the more ordinary demands of life because of his involvement in his work. We know, too, that there were times when he went out of his way to demonstrate his ability to cope with the more ordinary demands of life. The laziness is perhaps harder to explain but could be seen as part of the same tendency. Probably Orwell meant to suggest the writer's inclination to withdraw from the kind of routine activities that ordinary men and women tackle every day. Again, his acute self-awareness and his refusal to absolve himself led him to go to great lengths to avoid this withdrawal, and at times to overcompensate for the fact that he succumbed.

Thus the apparent paradoxes of Orwell the man emerge and can be understood as part of a remarkable man who was aware that in many ways he was different from others yet had no wish to exploit the fact except in terms of the effectiveness of his writing. The man who is present in Orwell's writing is acutely sensitive but has no wish to take advantage of his position as a writer, yet has to, in order to write at all. "Writing a book is a horrible, exhausting struggle, like a long bout of some painful illness." An odd thing to say, immediately after stating that writers are selfish and lazy. But the selfishness and laziness apply not to writing but to ordinary living. Writing itself involves making immense demands on oneself—and the demands impose selfishness in other spheres. "One would never undertake such a thing if one were not driven on by some demon whom one can neither resist nor understand." In other words, the motives are not just vanity. That is not enough to explain a writer's impulses or his capacity for endurance. What is the difference between the wish to communicate strong feelings, or the belief that one has something important to say, and the conviction that there is something one *must* say? Orwell writes that the demon cannot be resisted or understood, but the whole essay "Why I Write" is an attempt to explain that demon, in a sense to take that demon out of mythology, out of the rarefied atmosphere of artistic creativity, and give it a shape that has a toughly immediate reality. Writers are attention seekers, perhaps, and are rather better at getting attention than most people, but there are also, at least in Orwell's case, very particular reasons for writing which can be explained much more satisfactorily than the attribution of "the instinct that makes a baby squall for attention" suggests. And Orwell explains them.

Finally in this passage, and perhaps most interestingly for us, Orwell talks of the constant struggle "to efface one's own personality." Did Orwell really mean this? There is a very strong current of personality communicated in his writing. There is his frankness, his frequently disarming honesty, his directness of expression, his impatience, an occasional tetchiness, his open and pleasured response to a great range of human activities and experiences, his matter-of-fact ("laid back" is perhaps the appropriate contemporary phrase) reaction to overwhelming events—all this is present in his writing. If Orwell was really trying to efface his own personality, he either failed, or succeeded so well that he is presenting a totally reconstructed personality in his writing. But if that is the case the evidence suggests that he presented the same reconstructed personality in his letters, his diaries, and to his friends and acquaintances. What Orwell did in his writing, and what he was aiming to do, was to *control* his personality, rather than efface it. Literature without personality is rarely worth reading.

With this serving as a kind of introduction, we can now turn our attention to some of the shaping influences in his life. And again, it is only fair to use Orwell himself as our guide—so long as we bear in mind the problems that Orwell himself has drawn our attention to. His background was of a very particular kind. He was born in Bengal, and although he had virtually no childhood experience of India his Anglo-Indian origins stamped him deeply. His imperialist background went back several generations, with a great-great-grandfather a plantation owner in Jamaica. His grandfather was a Church of England minister in India and Tasmania, his father a minor official in the Indian civil service. His parents experienced the classic displacement of Anglo-Indians returning to Britain. They left a country where they had a function and an authority to take up their lives in a country where they had very little of either. This must have contributed to Orwell's acute sensitivity toward class. The clash between expectations and reality suffered by members of the middle classes who were not at all sure where they were or what they should be doing is a strong current in Orwell's writing.

Orwell was given a traditional upper middle-class education, as if his parents were confident of who they were and what their son should be. But Orwell himself seemed to be without this confidence, at least outside the context of the family home. His refusal, or inability, to accept a class definition of his identity and function caused him much unhappiness, but when, after a period at the prep school he describes in "Such, Such Were the Joys" he went as a scholarship boy to Eton, which represented the summit of elitist education, he found a more congenial—probably because more tolerant—environment, although in later years he was reluctant to admit this. He was certainly very conscious of the fact that he was not one of Eton's "moneyed young beasts," as he would describe them, but neither was he the only scholarship boy. Eton was more congenial not because the status and privilege that he found there were to his taste, but because there was room for unconventionality. And unconventionality became Eric Blair's chosen way of dealing with the problem of his origins in a decaying and uncertain middle-class territory.

One of the most insistent features of Blair/Orwell throughout his life and writing career is his hatred of orthodoxy. Eton almost certainly fed this, because it provided both an orthodoxy to kick against and space to do the kicking. Orwell vented his most scathing comments on the orthodoxies of class, of political ideologies, of religion, of nationality, and sometimes his remarks were both sweeping and unjust. His deep suspicion of orthodoxy made him wary of taking any of the accepted roads his background might have suggested, of joining a political party or any group that put group allegiance before individual commitment, of accepting current or fashionable views. It meant that he had a tendency to be idiosyncratic simply in order to avoid being the same. And if he did accept a view that was held by more than a very few others he found it necessary to explain and justify his position, to demonstrate that he had arrived there independently, and usually to make it clear that he had all kinds of reservations, or that his reasons for going along with that particular view were not the same as other peoples'. This need to disassociate himself from the crowd was more than an intellectual trait. It was a radical part of his personality. The word *orthodoxy* recurs in his writing, and in Orwell's vocabulary it is a bad word.

Why then did he accept the "orthodoxy" of his background and enter the imperial service, which he did in 1922, going out to Burma to join the police force? It is a question that has often been asked. It is perhaps less important to suggest an answer than to point out that it illustrates another significant feature of Orwell's makeup, and that he took great pains later to make it clear that he was not an orthodox policeman. Orwell was always inclined to do what on the surface seemed least likely. Given the personality that had emerged at Eton, a sensitive, intelligent but awkward boy, not much of a joiner, the active participation in putting into practice British imperialist rule is hardly what might have been expected of the eighteen-year-old Orwell. It seems unlikely that he was forced into it by family tradition, although family tradition clearly suggested the possibility; more likely that even at that age Eric Blair, in rejecting one kind of orthodoxy, which would have indicated a spell at Oxford or Cambridge, half deliberately chose another. To test himself? To find out for himself what it was really like? (He must have been curious about this aspect of his inheritance.) To explore what he could be fairly sure would be an alienating experience? Did he have muckraking motives? Probably all of these played a part. It may look like a drastic step, but hindsight tells us it was characteristic.

Later it would provide material for some of Orwell's best writing, for "A Hanging" and "Shooting an Elephant," and also for one of his less good novels, *Burmese Days*. Both the good and the not-so-good are significant. The short pieces show the careful adoption of a certain kind of authorial stance which we now recognize as characteristic. The detached presence of a narrator who is at the same time deeply implicated in what is being related was something that Orwell worked hard at. It was probably this that he meant when he talked about the effacement of personality. Personality must not be allowed to intrude, to direct the account of events, but inevitably it is a part of events. Neither the author nor the reader should be allowed to retain the illusion that writing can be objective. In both "A Hanging" and "Shooting an Elephant," the writer is there. He is involved, he is implicated, he is human: his frailty is one of the things that both pieces are about. *Burmese Days* is very different. In many ways it is through fiction rather than nonfiction (or semi-fiction—it is not possible to resolve the problem of the fictional element in Orwell's nonfiction) that Orwell most directly gives shape to his own character and convictions. Fiction gave Orwell scope for a ruthlessness with himself and his experiences that could not exist elsewhere. Very likely *Burmese Days* had to be written. It was in that book, rather than in the more direct accounts, that Orwell worked the imperialist experience out of his system—except, of course, that he never succeeded in doing that and never wanted to do that. Masked in fiction, certain kinds of emotional and psychological responses could be activated. In nonfiction, or so it would seem, the mask is removed and the personality must be controlled. Some would argue that George Orwell was the mask of Eric Blair, but I would not agree.

Orwell had a natural respect for and a natural skepticism about human beings, whatever their class or race or religion, and throughout his life he neither condemned nor excused anyone except on individual grounds. In many people this would have been destroyed by the imperialist experience, because imperialist solidarity demands the suppression of any inclination to see a native population in individual terms. To see the underdog as a human being immediately made the imperialist position vulnerable. Yet Orwell understood solidarity and its attractions. And there was a moment, perhaps even a period, in his life when he embraced it. Of all his books *Homage to Catalonia*, his account of Spain in 1937 and his participation in the Civil War and his witnessing of the suppression of POUM, perhaps tells us the most about the more important things in his life. It is on the first page of that book that he describes a momentary encounter with an Italian militiaman. It is worth quoting at length.

He was a tough-looking youth of twenty-five or six, with reddish-yellow hair and powerful shoulders. His peaked leather cap was pulled fiercely over one eye. He was standing in profile to me, his chin on his breast, gazing with a puzzled frown at a map which one of the officers had open on the table. Something in his face deeply moved me. It was the face of a man who would commit murder and throw away his life for a friend—the kind of face you would expect in an Anarchist, though as likely as not he was a Communist. There were both candour and ferocity in it; also the pathetic reverence that illiterate people have for their supposed superiors. Obviously he could not make head nor tail of the map; obviously he regarded map-reading as a stupendous intellectual feat. I hardly know why, but I have seldom seen anyone—any man, I mean—to whom I have taken such an immediate liking. While they were talking round the table some remark brought it out that I was a foreigner. The Italian raised his head and said quickly:

'*Italiano?*'

I answered in my bad Spanish: '*No, Ingles. Y tu?*'

'*Italiano.*'

As we went out he stepped across the room and gripped my hand very hard. Queer the affection you can feel for a stranger! It was as though his spirit and mine had momentarily succeeded in bridging the gulf of language and tradition and meeting in utter intimacy. I hoped he liked me as well as I liked him. But I also knew that to retain my first impression of him I must not see him again; and needless to say I never did see him again. One was always making contacts of that kind in Spain.

This happened eight years after Orwell had come back from Burma, where he had had five years which, so far as we can tell, had been largely without warm and creative contact with like-minded people. He had lived with a vast gulf between himself and the Burmese which efforts to learn the language and to avoid stereoscopic vision could not overcome. Any sense of a collective spirit was impossible, unless he were to identify with the British Empire. The experience probably altered the way he looked back on Eton and encouraged him to think of himself as a loner. He fostered that aspect of himself, and it may have contributed to his choice of an essentially lonely occupation. But from time to time we can detect the emergence of a need to belong. Spain in 1937 was so important because Orwell experienced, perhaps for the first time, a gut feeling of belonging. He was able to sample a collective experience to some extent in wartime Britain, but by that time the instinctive reaction against collective feeling, the collective will, was highly developed and had become a part of his professional stance.

It is worth pausing over the passage I have quoted. The Italian militiaman is someone who on the surface would appear to have nothing in common with Orwell. He is tough, uneducated, from a country Orwell had never visited and speaking a language Orwell did not know. They were drawn together by commitment, by the sharing of a particular moment of a heightened experience, but most of all by a mutual recognition of what Orwell calls "utter intimacy." The chemistry was as profound and unexplainable as falling in love. It has an intense reality yet is terribly fragile. The magic would be destroyed if they were to meet again. For Orwell it symbolized the short-lived solidarity that the Spanish Civil War introduced him to for the first time. Solidarity was one thing, collectivity another. It was a crucial experience.

The language itself is equally revealing. The account is characteristically precise and matter-of-fact. There is nothing obviously attractive about the Italian—in fact, Orwell is at pains to draw attention to features that might put many people off, or at least be regarded as unappealing. The emotion of the moment had a great deal to do with the fact that the larger circumstances of the occasion translated the experience onto a plane that the details would never have suggested. Orwell is a master at this in his prose, presenting with sober lack of emotion a series of observed details or facts, and then releasing almost as an aside a sudden charge of emotional current or implied significance. Here at the same time he treats his own emotion—"Something in his face deeply moved me"—as an observed fact, taking its place in the paragraph along with everything else. The trademark of Orwell's personal documentary is this observation of himself.

We have jumped several years. If he had not learned it at Eton, Orwell learned in Burma to expect isolation. We can interpret this as a defense mechanism—it does not really matter. What does matter is the way it affected his manner of living and writing from 1928, when he left the Burma police and embarked on a career as a writer, having had, he explained, vague intentions of writing for some time. Having made the decision, Orwell set about putting it into effect with dogged and careful persistence.

Orwell's need to write was probably as much a need to work out an individually directed purpose in life as a need to express himself. In fact, the two things are inseparable. The self-expression and self-direction in Orwell's case went together. Orwell had to learn to write. His style is a learnt style, the result of practice and application: it did not bubble naturally out of a spring of talent. And because it is a learnt style the care and crafting that went into it are identifiable. Orwell's discarding of the muddling embellishments of language has been much remarked on. He tried to discard the muddling embellishments of life in much the same way. And this leads us to another insistent feature of his life. Along with the resistance to orthodoxy went the need for displacement, the need to take himself out of what he saw as a gray and decaying background, of his privileged schooling, his collusion with imperialism, and place himself in the midst of something, perhaps anything, quite different. But of course it wasn't just anything. Orwell chose to associate with the underside of mainstream existence, he was not forced there by necessity—although it was important that he believed that it was necessary, and the strength of psychological need was perhaps as powerful as any material necessity.

Did Orwell deliberately set out to touch rock bottom in Paris and London in order to mitigate his middle classness? In order to rub off some of the well-bred edges? In order to find out how the other half lived, a purely sociological curiosity? In order to do some kind of penance for his semi-privileged life and his career as imperialist policeman? There was probably something of all these involved in this period of his life. In *Wigan Pier* he includes a section of autobiography, in which he says:

I was conscious of an immense weight of guilt that I had got to expiate. I suppose that sounds exaggerated; but if you do for five years a job that you thoroughly disapprove of, you will probably feel the same. . . . I felt that I had got to escape not merely from imperialism but from every form of man's dominion over man. I wanted to submerge myself, to get right down among the oppressed, to be one of them and on their side against their tyrants. And, chiefly because I had had to think everything out in solitude, I had carried my hatred of oppression to extraordinary lengths. At that time failure seemed to me to be the only virtue. Every suspicion of self-advancement, even to 'succeed' in life to the extent of making a few hundreds a year, seemed to me spiritually ugly, a species of bullying.

Success as a writer certainly came slowly, and in the early years Orwell made very little money. It was important that he should balance such success as did come his way by maintaining a minimal existence, whether as a *plongeur* in the infested kitchens of Paris restaurants or as a tramp at rest in the joyless spikes of southern England. And he would do this in different ways for the rest of his life, never taking the easy road to any goal, never accepting the comfortable rewards that success might have brought him, never allowing himself to believe that he had earned the right to make fewer demands on himself. When after the war he was typing the final version of *Nineteen Eighty-Four* on the remote island of Jura, it was almost with a note of self-satisfaction that he explained that he had had to do it, ill as he was, because it was impossible to bring a typist to the island. Once again he had succeeded in overcoming a largely self-imposed difficulty. His kindliness and gentleness coexisted with an uncompromising attitude to himself and to those around him. If at times this seems harsh, even intolerant, sometimes downright silly—some of his dismissive comments on left-wing intellectuals are an example—remember that he was harder on himself than on anyone else, and also that he was never afraid to admit his mistaken judgments, and to retract if he felt that was right.

So Orwell learned what it was like to exist in appalling conditions, to go without food, to suffer acute physical discomfort of a very basic kind, to associate with people who were filthy and smelly and degraded. And he learned how to write about these things. As well as learning the techniques of writing, he had to learn what to write about and the form his writing should take. He was experimenting with fiction, but the demands and constraints of nonfiction were probably the best training he could put himself through. He wrote best when he was assembling observed detail, observed experience, including his own experience, whether in fiction or nonfiction. One of the reasons that his fiction is not to the taste of all readers is that Orwell's imagination was rooted in reality and on occasion let him down. There are occasions when fiction requires that the creative writer's imagination take off from reality, and that rarely happens in Orwell's writing. His imagination was not inspirational. It worked on what was in front of him.

Let us go back to Orwell's need for displacement. Having decided to be a writer it was not necessary for him to go about it in the way he did, whatever the need to discover what he should be writing about (and he must already have been clear that he did not want to write about conventional middle-class experience). He wanted to declass, deracinate himself, to take himself out of an environment in which he did not wish to feel at home. One might perhaps suggest that he determined to make a positive out of a negative, to transform what it is fair to interpret as the negative isolation of Burma into the creative isolation of Paris and London and Wigan, to make a virtue of necessity—except that it wasn't, in a material sense, a necessity. Orwell did not turn romantically to the oppressed. His wish to "submerge himself," as he put it, was not in the spirit of the left-wing intellectuals whom he despised, embracing the cause of the working classes and announcing that if it was working-class it was good. He went out of his way to make it clear, particularly in *Wigan Pier*, that there was a great deal about working-class existence and working-class men and women that he did not at all care for. And so he opened himself to accusations from all possible sides. He was a middle-class snooper who didn't understand the working classes; he was a middle-class renegade. Having set out down a lonely road, Orwell's writings removed a number of possibilities of comradeship.

It would be a mistake to think that Orwell was not vulnerable to such reactions. There are not many clues to his vulnerability, but there are some. In his letters—writing again—he generally sustained the personality of his writing for publication. In his dealings with women we can get hints that, like most of us, he needed love, warmth, and security, and that he had no wish, really, to exist in a totally isolated position, unaccepted on all sides. But the impression is very strong that he would not have been prepared to compromise his convictions in order to make personal gains.

Orwell was, then, a sensitive and vulnerable person who chose a lonely road. He chose an isolating profession, that of writer, and set about achieving his goals in such a way that he was, certainly at times, even more isolated than he need have been. He rejected any easy ways there might have been for an old Etonian who was not without literary and other useful contacts; at the same time the literary contacts did help him. Perhaps that made it even more important that he should avoid conventional literary territory in his subject matter. Not that he was a pioneer. There had been others before him who had entered the world of the underprivileged and written about it, notably Jack London. But in the 1930s it was fashionable to make laudatory comments about the working classes with little idea of the realities of working-class life, and Orwell was not going to associate himself with that kind of thing. Some would say that he did not understand the working classes—perhaps he understood the nonworking classes, the tramps and down-and-outs and rejects rather better. But at least he was prepared for experience not just investigation. The doing was the justification of the writing.

The early thirties were the years of discovery and training. He forged a style of such quality and authority that it has generated its own adjective—Orwellian. He learned the "virtues" of failure. He found out about at least one area of experience that he could write about and that he felt it was important to write about.

But characteristic of Orwell's style is a vein of alienation, and it is a feature of the man also. He submerged himself, perhaps, but he did not merge—he did not embrace the depths and become one with the oppressed. He was a writer, and as a writer he kept his distance. His brief was not to *become* a tramp or a miner or one of the unemployed, but to stand as witness to their lives. But the experience was alienating, and so was the writing. To cope with it Orwell had to develop a style that accommodated himself, that absorbed into its fabric the ego of the observer, that could render the observer one of the observed. That is the most striking quality of *Down and Out in Paris and London* and the feature that stamped his nonfiction until the end of his career.

The alienation went with the vast gulf Orwell saw between the real and, not the ideal, but the acceptable. "It is not possible for any thinking person to live in such a world as ours without wanting to change it," he wrote in a letter to Stephen Spender. Such a remark tells us two very important things about Orwell. First, that he had a commitment to changing society, but also that he had the ability to make the most extraordinary generalizations with total conviction, with the result that even if we know that they can't be true we have an equally strong sense that they should be true. Of course there were, when Orwell made that comment, "thinking" people who complacently led their lives without any serious wish, let alone action, to change the world. However, if this remark of Orwell's wasn't true, the conviction is such that we feel it should have been true. The effect of Orwell's directness of style is such as to make us grasp the truth of the intention.

As Orwell himself was to say later, the Spanish Civil War was the crucial experience of his life, both politically and creatively. It gave him an understanding of the potential of revolution, and of the catastrophe and pain of betrayal. It gave him a vital opportunity for action, which, amongst other things, allowed the dormant practical experience of policing in Burma to make a contribution to the enactment of belief. And Orwell relished the practicalities. This is an important part of the man he was. Whether it was skinning a rabbit, digging the garden, smoking a kipper, or handling an out-of-date rifle, he enjoyed the doing, and made it clear that being a writer did not mean that he was out of touch with either ordinary everyday doing or the more resonant, if not actually more dramatic, activities of war. In Spain the motivations blended. If Orwell had struggled in his apprenticeship years to weld art and life together, in Spain art and life without any effort on his part seemed to become as one. The motivations of action were the same as the motivations of writing. He became a political animal without ceasing to be a writer.

He retained his suspicion of political parties—political parties could not be detached from dreaded orthodoxy. He took his own individual, and again at times isolated, route in the direction of socialism, and took it upon himself not only to further the socialist cause but to alert socialists in particular to the internal dangers that beset it. The times, he would say later, forced him to become a propagandist. "I hate writing that kind of stuff," he wrote, "and am much more interested in my own experiences, but unfortunately in this bloody period we are living in one's own experiences *are* being mixed up in controversies, intrigues etc."

The experience of Spain was in one way a wonderful coalescence, and it produced, in *Homage to Catalonia*, his best nonfiction work, where he coped most clearly and confidently and creatively with his personality as well as the events he was describing. But it also left him cultivating, even more assiduously than before, a determined pessimism. He forced himself and others to look at the grimmest realities: the concentration camps in Germany, and the other horrors of fascism, the certainty of war and its likely effects, and so on.

In stripping himself of any chance of evasion, of head-in-the-sand protection, he stripped others. His foresight was not used as a kind of exemption. He communicates so strongly because he demonstrates that he himself is facing these realities without flinching; in fact, as some felt he did with the tramps, there are times when he takes himself unnecessarily close to them.

It was in this spirit that Orwell prepared himself for the coming war. For a brief period he was a member of the I.L.P., the Independent Labour Party, which was pacifist. But it became manifestly clear that a war against fascism had to be fought and that such a war could not be a matter of megalomaniac leaders slugging it out. The people had to participate, and in that participation, Orwell, like many others, saw an immense potential for change. He had been wounded in Spain, and was not well, and was profoundly frustrated at not being able to contribute directly to the war effort. But it meant that he wrote as never before, attentively, purposefully, with care—the care applying not only to the words he chose but to the quality of his observation. It was as if wartime Britain, in both its sense of emergency and its dreariness, highlighted the significance of the tiniest observable details, and many of these details found their way into Orwell's writing, and are an essential part of its and his character.

Orwell was never carried away by the surge and excitement of large ideas. For him there was no magic in rhetoric—on the contrary, rhetoric was to be distrusted, and he sought to demythologize it. One of the ways in which he fortified himself against the temptations of grandiloquent solutions was by paying great attention to the smallest details of living, the details that most intimately contributed to the fabric of existence. The "As I Please" column that he began writing for the *Tribune* newspaper in 1943 gave him just the outlet he needed for weaving together these threads of experience, and they contribute significantly to our understanding of Orwell the man. For example, and this is picked quite at random, he writes about the problems of dishwashing: "Every time I wash up a batch of crockery I marvel at the unimaginativeness of human beings who can travel under the sea and fly through the cloud, and yet have not known how to eliminate this sordid time-wasting drudgery from their daily lives." Domestic appliances, according to Orwell, have scarcely changed since the Bronze Age, and "If our methods of making war had kept pace with our methods of keeping house, we should be just about on the verge of discovering gunpowder."

This kind of thing tells us a great deal about Orwell. First, that he considered dish-washing an appropriate and serious subject and understood the implications of domestic drudgery. Secondly, he makes it clear that he is writing out of his own experience and, incidentally, provides us with another example of a man rejecting and seeking a solution to what women have tended to accept. What is equally interesting is that in suggesting solutions it does not occur to Orwell that a machine might be the answer. Inevitably this entire piece is resonant with premonitions of *Nineteen Eighty-Four*. He talks of burst pipes and the problems of rubbish disposal, wartime discomforts. These details of the drabness of existence look forward to the blocked sinks and out-of-order elevators in Victory Mansions. The fact that Orwell's vision of 1984 is conspicuously without labor-saving devices may be due as much to Orwell's lack of a technological imagination as to his contention that the "revolution" he describes has brought little benefit to the ordinary lives of ordinary people.

What is pertinent to a discussion of Orwell the man is that he paid attention to these small and, to some, trivial details, saw them as inescapable ingredients of life, contributing radically to its shape and texture. And we find this tendency throughout his writing. Orwell knew about the misery of not being able to keep warm, or keep clean, of the trials of survival amidst the bomb debris of wartime London, and he knew how these basic features could shape human existence. He also understood that no amount of observation would supply what could be learned from experience, and that no amount of secondhand retelling could make up for direct observation. On a number of occasions he comments on something he has heard and makes a note to himself in passing that he must check it out. It must also be said that Orwell, with this understanding, did not allow the physical delineations of his existence to dictate *his* life: he went on writing, in spite of every possible adverse circumstance, and never was he so productive as through the war years. Now is the moment to emphasize his sheer determination.

It would be a mistake to give the impression that "As I Please" was preoccupied with the more sordid aspects of daily existence. He writes about books and bombs, socialism and snobbery, revolution and realism, pubs and propaganda—anything and everything that he writes about anywhere else, but in "As I Please" it is woven together into an extraordinarily rich, diverse, and enjoyable fabric. Perhaps most delightful are his comments, so often disarmingly unexpected, on such topics as rose bushes, toads, and bird watching in central London. As he pointed out himself in his column for January 21, 1944, in reply to a criticism that he was too negative, "I like praising things, when there is anything to praise." The column was, after all, called "As I Please," and it does convey considerable pleasure. It is required reading for all those whose vision of Orwell is of a gloomy pessimist who was so convinced of the inevitability of disaster that he was blind to the good things in life. Quite the contrary was true. However depressed Orwell became about the present, however pessimistic about the future, he was always able to see something in the life around him that aroused his interest and pleasure.

He distrusted the sophisticated: sophistication was too readily used to gloss over artificiality. His pleasures were simple. He asked very little in the way of personal gratification, enjoyed making a virtue of necessity. It has often been said that he was old-fashioned in his pleasures, indeed in his view of the way life should be. There was something unrealistically pastoralist, preindustrial, something almost William Morris-like, about Orwell's vision of humankind at one with work and the world. The nostalgia of *Coming Up for Air*, for example, has often been remarked on, with the suggestion that in harking back to the apparently peaceful pre-1914 world Orwell was forgetting that the equilibrium was based on class, privilege, and imperialism. But Orwell does not suggest that he wished to reconstruct the prewar environment, only that much had been lost that was of value. His nostalgia is part of a larger theme concerning the overwhelming of the natural by the artificial.

Something of Orwell's vision of the good and the pleasurable can be seen in this passage from *Wigan Pier*, which reverberates with some of the values Orwell considered essential. He contends that a working-class home, a home, that is, where at least the menfolk were in work, is "warm, decent, deeply human," and goes on:

> home life seems to fall . . . into a sane and comely shape. I have often been struck by the peculiar easy completeness, the perfect symmetry as it were, of a working-class interior at its best. Especially on winter evenings after tea, when the fire glows in the open range and dances mirrored in the steel fender, when Father, in shirt-sleeves, sits in the rocking chair at one side of the fire reading the racing finals, and Mother sits on the other with her sewing, and the children are happy with a pennorth of mint humbugs, and the dog lolls roasting himself on the rag mat—it is a good place to be in, provided that you can be not only in it but sufficiently *of* it to be taken for granted.

From the standpoint of 1984 we can of course easily detect the flaws, the caricaturing of class and gender roles. But let us look at this not as a description of the actual or even of the desirable, but as a reflection of Orwell's own needs. The language is revealing: "comely shape," "symmetry," the sense of ease and balance and contentment, each individual relaxed and untroubled in an allotted place, and, by implication, Orwell there too, of it as well as in it. It is quite clear that hand in hand with his powerful and to some extent self-imposed sense of isolation went a profound need to belong, to find a comfortable place in the right environment. Perhaps it was the search for the right environment that led him to the remote island of Jura, where he almost ended his days.

How did he appear to his friends and acquaintances? Here is Geoffrey Gorer, talking about meeting him in 1935:

> I found he was one of the most interesting people I've ever known, I was never bored in his company. He was interested in nearly everything. And his attitudes were original. He didn't take accepted ideas. . . . I would have said he was an unhappy man. He was too big for himself. I suppose if he'd been younger you would have said "coltish." He was awfully likely to knock things off tables, to trip over things. I mean, he was a gangling, physically badly coordinated young man. I think his feelings that even the inanimate world was against him which he did have at some times, I mean any gas stove he had would go wrong, any radio would break down. . . . He was a lonely man—until he met Eileen [his first wife], a very lonely man. He was

fairly well convinced that nobody could like him, which made him prickly. It seems clear that marriage mellowed him. Some years later Tosco Fyvel met "an extremely tall, thin man, looking more than his years, with gentle eyes and deep lines that hinted at suffering on his face. The word 'saint' was used by one of his friends and critics after his death, and—well—perhaps he had a touch of this quality. Certainly there was nothing of the fierce pamphleteer in his personal manner. He was awkward, almost excessively mild."

Women found him attractive, yet it was a woman friend of his wife who commented on the fact that "work was more important than any personal relationship": it is fairly clear that he cannot have been easy to live with, and equally clear that Eileen was rather a remarkable person. "All writers are vain, selfish and lazy." Yes, Orwell had the vanity of a man who believed himself to be right. He was gentle and mild, but without humility. He was selfish, in the way that any writer almost has to be, in order to be able to work, although Orwell never claimed any privileges for creativity. Creativity had to take its chance along with other kinds of human activity. It was the sense of obligation that he had to write—the demon—that made Orwell put work before people. And yet to suggest that he was uncaring would of course be nonsensical. He wrote because he cared.

Orwell himself had a strong sense of the shape life ought to have. This sense is present in that passage from *Wigan Pier*, but present also, sometimes in an almost offhand kind of way, in most of what he wrote. He could hammer out his conviction in certain values, in decency, equality, comeliness, but he was just as likely to suggest obliquely that these were what mattered. The force of his writing is such that it is not possible to remove the man from the environment that he himself created, and placed George Orwell in. More than anything else we see Orwell in a world of things, of solid objects, a tangible, three-dimensional environment, sensuously powerful in a most radical way. In Orwell's writing things are as important as ideas, and that was true of his life also. Things have a vital reality. He lavishes affection and care on them. And things could be, and perhaps more often than not for most people were and are, simple and ordinary and knowable. Things are plain, ideas are fancy, and Orwell was a plain man. Things can be trusted (although they are vulnerable, as *Nineteen Eighty-Four* demonstrates); with ideas you have to be watchful. As Orwell demonstrated, language is both volatile and vulnerable, and you cannot have ideas without language. But things have their own life. Bernard Crick has called Orwell's feeling for objects a "piety towards things." It seems to me to explain a great deal. The spiritual and intellectual inventions of humankind had in Orwell's lifetime reached a horrific climax—and we have now taken them further. It would be impossible to question the validity of Orwell's insistence on the moral value of certain kinds of reality and on its essential supports—plainness of language and decency of behavior. We may never be able to explain the complexities of Eric Blair/George Orwell, or resolve the contradictions that are largely the result of his own honesty. But we can be quite sure that the man and his message are inseparable.

The Englishness of George Orwell

by Peter Stansky

This is Orwell's year, and the western world is celebrating. Actuality, at least in the sense of the calendar, is catching up with fiction. Both 1984, the year, and *Nineteen Eighty-Four*, the novel, are upon us.

A question in my mind is whether in 1985 and thereafter a novel about the future that has as its title a date in the past will affect the book's readership. Up to now, the book has had an astounding number of readers, in the tens of millions, which has effectively removed the text from consideration of ordinary literature into almost a special genre of its own. The spurt of interest starting with the fall of 1983 has been intense: a science fiction conference in Antwerp which has the book as its theme; a more staid conference at the home of the Council of Europe in Strasbourg; a conference at the Smithsonian in Washington emphasizing the future; another in Washington concerned with the past and the man; and the present gathering of scholars and critics at the Library of Congress at the end of April, the month in which the book begins: "It was a bright cold day in April, and the clocks were striking thirteen,"[1] is the famous first sentence of the book. Various collections of essays are being published on the book and the year, one edited by myself for the *Portable Stanford* series and the publisher W. H. Freeman. The seventieth printing of the mass paperback has a special introduction by Walter Cronkite. This, to my mind, is a nice irony, as Cronkite's position on the American television screen has been almost that of an anti-Big Brother—virtually ubiquitous before his retirement, but designed to be reassuring rather than threatening. Oxford University Press is issuing a special edition of the text. One begins to suspect overkill, and it wouldn't be surprising if there were an anti-reaction and a certain tiredness in response to Orwell and *Nineteen Eighty-Four* in 1985.

Surveys of the book and of the life of the man will be available, perhaps overly available, during this year. What I should like to do here is to dwell on a somewhat more general consideration, or theme, in Orwell's life which is of special interest to a historian, particularly to a historian of modern Britain such as myself: Orwell's Englishness. It is essential to an understanding of the man and his intention in writing *Nineteen Eighty-Four*. And it is not an aspect of his life that will concern those who are likely to use the book as a jumping off point, or pretext, for an assessment of today's world and the world of the future. Thus, one television show has recently claimed—I don't know quite how justified the claim—that there are 130 predictions in *Nineteen Eighty-Four* and 120 of them have already come true. Those discussed proved to be mostly in the area of surveillance.

My intention in this paper is to examine the background for Orwell's achievement, which in a literal and sad sense climaxed in *Nineteen Eighty-Four*. It was the last book he published, in June 1949, seven months before his death of tuberculosis in January 1950, at the tragically early age of 46. I hope that such a discussion may be helpful not only for a better understanding of Orwell himself, but also that it may illuminate some aspects of the English character, and the nature of political and social change in England.

It is a cliché about English society, emphasized by those photographs of dark-suited, bowler-hatted English gentlemen walking along with their tightly furled umbrellas in a street in the City of London, that it is made up of conformists. It is another cliché that the education in boarding schools, the so-called public schools, provide that sort of privileged education dedicated to furthering conformity. Yet the society that created the public schools at the same time produces brilliant mavericks who are out to use existing institutions for aims of their own. Up through the eighteenth century the English had a reputation for being unruly, and a vast historical literature exists on the transformation of their society, how it was made more orderly as it sustained those traumatic shocks at the end of the eighteenth century that transformed England into the first modern nation. I've always felt that under the veneer of good manners and restraint, English society is prone to disorder. Hence, strong institutions are needed to tame it. For most Englishmen and women, such institutions work as they are intended to do. But the brilliant exceptions, the mavericks, both violate and use those institutions, perhaps at a considerable psychic price to themselves.

One only has to think of the two greatest prime ministers of the nineteenth century—William Gladstone and Benjamin Disraeli—and the two greatest prime ministers of the twentieth century—David Lloyd George and Winston Churchill—to realize that those who have succeeded politically in the most overwhelming way in Britain have tended to be mavericks and were intensely hated and distrusted by the more tradition-bound and conventional elements in the land. The fulminations against those four men that took place at the dinner tables of the great and the good would have convinced any eavesdropper that they were considered mad. All four violated the traditions of their society in order to preserve it. William Gladstone became increasingly radical as he grew older and busily upset the old ways of the universities, the civil service, the army, the electorate, and the church, all to create a society which to his mind would be closer to one that was serving God. Disraeli, Jew, dandy, novelist, tory democrat, supporter of the Chartists, became the representative of the "gentlemen of England" and the great inspiration of that tradition of modern Toryism, now apparently being abandoned by Mrs. Thatcher. Lloyd

George and Churchill helped preserve their country during the two devastating wars of this century. Each of them was deeply distrusted by almost all their fellow politicians. Both began as social radicals out to transform society, although they were much less radical than they were thought to be. Only the fact that the country was in a terrible state in the middle of the First World War, and on the verge of defeat in the first year of the Second World War, forced the more traditional politicians to turn to these "wild men," seeing them as unfortunate necessities at a time of extreme peril.

And yet, with the possible exception of Lloyd George, each of the four great prime ministers was deeply wedded to the nation's institutions and determined to strengthen them as best he could, but—a most significant *but*—according to his own conceptions, which were very reluctantly accepted by others. As a "character type," Orwell belongs among the mavericks. A writer and artist who succeeded brilliantly in his chosen career, he was never a highly active political figure, and he had no wish to be. Yet he was a relentless political commentator and in his life and in his writing he had, I believe, quite a few resemblances to the four great men of politics.

Of the four, Lloyd George, as an outsider and a Welshman, had the least respect for English institutions. Gladstone, the son of an extremely successful Liverpool merchant, was perfectly happy to fulfill his father's wishes that he become a member of the English Establishment through education (Eton and Christ Church, Oxford) and through marriage (to Catherine Glynn, a member of an old and rich Whig family). Although eventually he would be regarded by many as a man out to destroy traditional English society, Gladstone always saw himself as its defender. Benjamin Disraeli couldn't have been more of an outsider, but his aim was to penetrate into the heart of the English world, while not sacrificing any element of his colorful personality. Winston Churchill, a grandson of the duke of Marlborough, certainly an insider, was determined to use his connections for all they were worth, to establish a position and a point of view that was strongly his own.

Orwell was of course somewhat different from all these gentlemen, but not so different as one might think. Like Churchill, he too was descended from the aristocracy, as the great-great-great grandson of the earl of Westmorland. But apart from a family bible and a few mementoes, the noble connection was quite faint by the time Orwell was born in 1903, while it was very much present in Churchill's life from the moment of his birth in Blenheim Palace. But in their differing ways both men were born to families that had a strong tradition of serving, and profiting from, the state. In Churchill's case, the tradition began with his illustrious ancestor, the first duke of Marlborough, the great general and victor at Blenheim in 1704. In Orwell's case *his* ancestors, the earls of Westmorland, had been serving the state since 1624; the Westmorland grandfather of Lady Mary Fane, who married the wealthy Charles Blair, Orwell's great-grandfather, had been an officer under Marlborough and built the family's Palladian villa, Mereworth, in Kent near where

Orwell—or to use his real name, Eric Arthur Blair—would pick hops as part of his apprenticeship as a writer. (He made use of the experience in his novel *A Clergyman's Daughter*.) The Blair family did not serve England in so high-level or lucrative a way as the Westmorlands, but Thomas Blair, Orwell's grandfather, followed the more modest pursuit of a country clergyman, after having served God in the Empire. His parish was Milbourne St. Andrew in Dorset, and the position was given to him by his cousin, Lady Mary's niece's son, Gen. Sir John Michel. Although the Blairs may have originally been Scottish, this was the area in a beautiful part of southern England in which the family resided, perfectly respectably but not increasing the family fortune.

The tradition of service to the state continued in the next generation. Richard Walmesley Blair, a younger son of the Reverend Thomas Blair, spent his working life in the Opium Service in India, seeing to it that enough opium was grown to supply the highly profitable sale of the drug to China, a right which had been assured through the Opium Wars between Britain and China. Richard Blair made a late marriage to Ida Mabel Limouzin, half-French and half-English. They had three children, their son Eric surrounded by an older and a younger sister, Marjorie and Avril. It was for the son that the better education was reserved, but rather than sending the children home alone to attend school, Mrs. Blair returned with Marjorie and Eric (Avril was not yet born) from India in 1907, five years before Mr. Blair retired and came back to England permanently himself. Young Eric received a proper upbringing in the Thameside town of Henley, where his mother made sure that he played with the right children and did not pick up a wrong accent.

The crucial development, in terms of Orwell's relation to authority, was his being sent away to prep school in 1911, at the age of eight. The school was St. Cyprian's, on the South Coast at Eastbourne. Eric Blair was clearly a very bright boy, and he was accepted on a scholarship by Mr. and Mrs. Vaughan Wilkes, the proprietors of the school, on the assumption that he would go on to win a scholarship at an eminent public school—which he did, at Eton—and thus reflect credit upon St. Cyprian's. He was following the standard educational course of the English "lower-upper-middle class" (Orwell's own designation) and a course earlier followed by Gladstone and Churchill. Like Orwell at St. Cyprian's, Churchill was intensely unhappy at *his* prep school, St. George's, where beatings were administered by the sadistic headmaster, and his parents completely neglected him. Churchill, also like Orwell, had a better time at *his* public school, Eton's great rival, Harrow, but like Orwell, he decided (or had it decided for him) not to continue his education at one of the ancient universities. Instead, after training at Sandhurst, he went out to serve the Empire in the Army in India. Churchill was less reflective and introspective than Orwell; in any case he was more indubitably and securely in the upper classes. There is little evidence that he ever basically questioned, even in his reforming days, the social system of the country and its education in particular, no matter how unhappy he was at his boarding school from his eighth to his twelfth year.

Orwell's parallel schoolboy years produced the material for one of his minor masterpieces, the essay "Such, Such Were the Joys." Its title is an ironic use of a line from one of William Blake's "Songs of Innocence." Written late in his life, it was so libellous of Mrs. Vaughan Wilkes that it could not be published in England until 1968, after her death in her nineties. Yet despite his hatred of the school, Orwell acknowledged it was only doing its job in ramming facts into him and preparing him for the examinations which would take him to the next stage in the training of a proper member of the English ruling classes. He was at St. Cyprian's from 1911 to 1917; and, of course, during his last three years there, Britain was at war. Patriotism, especially in the first years of the war, was at its height. On the surface at least, and perhaps more profoundly, Orwell participated in the feeling of patriotic excitement. His first two publications, written while he was still at St. Cyprian's, appeared in his "hometown" newspaper *The Henley and South Oxfordshire Standard*. In the second month of the war, that paper printed a short poem of his, "Awake! Young Men of England!" Its concluding lines, rather awful as verse even perhaps from an eleven-year-old, were strong in sentiment, exhorting young men who were old enough to enlist. "For if, when your Country's in need, / You do not enlist by the thousand, / You truly are cowards indeed."[2] Two years later, on July 21, 1916, another one of his poems was published by the *Standard*: an elegy mourning Field Marshall Lord Kitchener, who had been drowned at sea. In his literary efforts, on the surface at least, he was certainly a conformist child.

But, like many clever children, there was also present in him a young cynic, a state of mind confirmed by his contemporary at St. Cyprian's and Eton, the man of letters, Cyril Connolly. Orwell imbibed an irreconcilable double message at the heart of his education:

> The essential conflict [at the school] was between the tradition of nineteenth-century asceticism and the actually existing luxury and snobbery of the pre-1914 age. On the one side were low-church Bible Christianity, sex puritanism, insistence on hard work, respect for academic distinction, disapproval of self-indulgence: on the other, contempt for "braininess" and worship of games, contempt for foreigners and the working class, an almost neurotic dread of poverty, and, above all, the assumption not only that money and privilege are things that matter, but that it is better to inherit them than to have to work for them. Broadly, you were bidden to be at once a Christian and a social success, which is impossible.[3]

Whatever the truth of the matter, his own feeling at the school was that he was despised there, most notably by the headmistress and by many of his fellow little boys, as one who was comparatively poor. The power of Mrs. Vaughan Wilkes and the capriciousness of her putting the little boys in and out of favor at her "court" are confirmed by a whole series of memoirs by others who attended or knew this hotbed of a prep school: Cyril Connolly, Cecil Beaton, Gavin Maxwell. Connolly in his *Enemies of Promise* (1948) writes about the school: "It was worldly and worshipped success, political and social; though Spartan, the death-rate was low, for it was well run and based on that stoicism which characterized the English governing class and which has since been under-estimated. 'Character, character, character.' "[4] Connolly described Orwell either at the end of this period at prep school or at the beginning of his time at Eton as a "true rebel" in contrast to himself; he knew *he* was a "stage" one. The school nurtured in Orwell a belief in his personal worthlessness. "The conviction that it was *not possible* for me to be a success went deep enough to influence my actions till far into adult life. Until I was about thirty I always planned my life on the assumption not only that any major undertaking was bound to fail, but that I could only expect to live a few years longer."[5]

Designed to produce conformists, these exclusive private schools, certainly in the case of Orwell, Gladstone, and Churchill, produced gifted young men ready to question their society. The paradox of Orwell—a very English paradox—was that although he was highly skeptical and prone to question the status quo, his background—as the son of a family that served the state—his education, and his class position indoctrinated him with a certain reverence for Britain, an engrained patriotism. Both attitudes were paralleled in the four prime ministers. These attitudes, which came naturally to Orwell, were not shared by many other prominent intellectual figures on the Left in the 1930s—most famously, the writers that clustered around W. H. Auden. They were much more likely to be children of the professional middle class with traditions less tied to serving the state. Their rebellious feelings reached an apogee at the time of the Second World War. Orwell himself went through a period of some confusion as the war drew nearer. For a while he was tempted by pacifism; then, vehemently and rather intolerantly, he rejected it. His attitude towards his country was nicely summed up in his short essay of the autumn, 1940, with its brilliant title "My Country, Right or Left." It concludes:

> I grew up in an atmosphere tinged with militarism, and afterwards I spent five boring years within the sound of bugles. To this day it gives me a faint feeling of sacrilege not to stand to attention during 'God Save the King'. That is childish, of course, but I would sooner have had that kind of upbringing than be like the left-wing intellectuals who are so 'enlightened' that they cannot understand the most ordinary emotions. It is exactly the people whose hearts have *never* leapt at the sight of a Union Jack who will flinch from revolution when the moment comes. . . . [There is] the possibility of building a Socialist on the bones of a [Colonel] Blimp, the power of one kind of loyalty to transmute itself into another, the spiritual need for patriotism and the military virtues, for which, however little the boiled rabbits of the Left may like them, no substitute has yet been found.[6]

This, of course, is Orwell at his most dogmatic and abrasive, but his feelings are clear.

A belief in an essential patriotism, along with a belief in an essential revolution, emerged also in *The Lion and the Unicorn*, the little book he wrote in 1941 during the worst of the Blitz. He had come to believe in a need for extraordinary transformations in Britain, even a revolution, if the war was to be won. As events proved, he was wrong, in part because of Churchill's abilities in leading the nation. Far fewer changes were necessary in the fabric of society than Orwell had predicted, although Britain did emerge from the war as a country ready for the transformations of the welfare state under the Labour government of 1945-50. But this was not the sort of total revolution that Orwell had hoped for. He wrote in *The Lion and the Unicorn*:

> This war, unless we are defeated, will wipe out most of the existing class privileges. There are every day fewer people who wish them to continue. Nor need we fear that as the pattern changes life in England will lose its peculiar flavour. The new red cities of Greater London are crude enough, but these things are only the rash that accompanies a change. . . . The intellectuals who hope to see [England] Russianized or Germanized will be disappointed. The gentleness, the hypocrisy, the thoughtlessness, the reverence of law and the hatred of uniforms will remain, along with the suet puddings and the misty skies. It needs some very great disaster, such as prolonged subjugation by a foreign enemy, to destroy a national culture. The Stock Exchange will be pulled down, the horse plough will give way to the tractor, the country houses will be turned into children's holiday camps, the Eton and Harrow match will be forgotten, but England will still be England, an everlasting animal stretching into the future and the past, and, like all living things, having the power to change out of recognition and yet remain the same.[7]

But that was in 1941. Although now a socialist, Orwell came to be positively Burkean in his belief in the conservative nature of change. He was supportive of what he saw as the eternal verities of English life even as he wished for radical and immediate change at the surface. After the war, in his two masterpieces, *Animal Farm* and *Nineteen Eighty-Four*, he was anxious to point out how socialism might become perverted and destroy what he valued most in the central aspects of English society: a respect for truth and the past, the virtue of common sense, the importance of privacy, and personal independence.

How did Orwell come to this position which reconciled him with the idea of authority in his own country—but an authority he wanted totally transformed? He was a rebel who believed, as did the four prime ministers, that they could now work with the established powers because it was they—the established powers—that had changed. Of course a crucial difference is that Orwell was a critic who never had power and hence was not identified, as the prime ministers were, with the state itself. Yet in the last five years of his life, he was closer to the "powers that be" than he had been at any other time previously. All five men were rebels of sorts who saw themselves as being dedicated to the most lasting and important values of their society, its eternal verities, which had been forgotten by their conformist fellow members of the ruling class but that might be found in more "ordinary" people.

The politicians were able to make an extraordinary appeal to the multitude and convey a great generosity of spirit. They were able to suggest that they were talking for and to those who were neglected by other politicians. One only has to remember the intense popularity of Gladstone, the "People's William," or Disraeli's posthumous role as the inspirer of the Tory popular organization, the Primrose League, or Lloyd George's vehement public speeches. As Churchill remarked about his own role during the war, he had been privileged to give the "roar" of the lion for his fellow countrymen. Orwell too saw himself as speaking for England, as far more in touch with and respectful of the point of view of ordinary English men and women than other intellectuals. In *The Road to Wigan Pier*, his 1937 report on the depressed state of the north of England, he emphasizes the need to identify with the ordinary person, as in his unforgettable glimpse of a poverty-stricken woman seen from a train, cleaning a drainpipe. He could identify with coal miners and with the working class, as in the almost Dickensian family picture he presents at the end of the first section of the book:

> Especially on winter evenings after tea, when the fire glows in the open range and dances mirrored in the steel fender, when Father, in shirt-sleeves, sits in the rocking chair at one side of the fire reading the racing finals, and Mother sits on the other with her sewing, and the children are happy with a pennorth of mint humbugs and the dog lolls roasting himself on the rag mat—it is a good place to be in, provided that you can be not only in it but sufficiently *of* it to be taken for granted.[8]

How had he reached this position of a reconciliation with society and with authority, so far from the downtrodden and bitter little school boy who left St. Cyprian's at the age of thirteen in 1917? At Eton from 1917 to 1922 he had mixed with the future leaders of his country, and most particularly, as he was a King's Scholar, with those who were the more intellectual among the students. Right after the First World War, Eton went through a somewhat "bolshevik" period with doubts about militarism and the sacrifice of so many old Etonians on the battlefields of France. So Orwell would have been both dubious about his country's values and, at the same time, imbued with them, while at Eton. The same rather schizophrenic experience awaited him, certainly in retrospect, when, after Eton, he went, in a manner of speaking, into the family business, and became a police officer in Burma, in the Indian Imperial Police. He came to hate his work, keeping the Burmese in order; and yet, unlike so many others who moved to the left, he did not idealize those who were oppressed; in fact he rather hated them. But he came to believe that the British had no right to rule other countries, and he asserted India's right to independence, should she wish it, at the time of the Second World War. The relationship with authority was most famously summed up in his brilliant essay of 1936, "Shooting an Elephant." The four prime ministers had spoken and written thousands, perhaps millions, of words on imperialism, its triumphs and tragedies, but its nature has probably never been so succinctly evoked as in Orwell's essay, which tells of his having to shoot a rogue elephant, once dangerous, now harmless, simply to keep face among the Burmese. That was the way a representative of empire was expected to act. Orwell could achieve the rare balance of both being an anti-imperialist without being sentimental about those under British rule. As he wrote, "The sole thought in my mind was that if anything went wrong those two thousand Burmans would see me pursued [by the elephant], caught, trampled on and reduced to a grinning corpse. . . . And if that happened it was quite probable that some of them would laugh. That would never do. There was only one alternative. I shoved the cartridges into the magazine and lay down on the road to get a better aim."[9]

In 1927 Orwell returned to England in order to become a writer, but also because, at least so it seemed to him when he wrote about the period fifteen years later, he could not bear to stay on and take part in an oppressive colonial system. The prime ministers never had quite such a squeamish attitude towards power, although Gladstone at the very beginning of his career resigned from the government over an issue of conscience. But however different, all these figures, with their complex relationship to authority, were anxious to transform it into something of which they could approve. The experience of being a police officer was so embittering for Orwell that he went "down and out" in Paris and England in order to purge himself of his guilt, the shame of having been a figure of authority in Burma. His novels of the 1930s, *Burmese Days*, *A Clergyman's Daughter*, *Keep the Aspidistra Flying*, are all about figures caught in the dilemma of coming to terms with the society in which they live, and which they don't approve of. John Flory in *Burmese Days* hates the role-playing imposed upon him as an English businessman in Burma and is driven to suicide; Dorothy Hare in *A Clergyman's Daughter* flees into amnesia in order to escape the role of a dutiful daughter that society expects her to play. She eventually returns to it when she recovers her memory, but with her faith destroyed, and her belief in what she is doing gone. Gordon Comstock, in *Keep the Aspidistra Flying*, tries to abandon the worship of the money god but accepts the obligations of ordinary existence when he gets his girlfriend pregnant and agrees to marry her—having a "stake" in society forces him to conform, even to placing an aspidistra in their living room, the ultimate symbol of lower middle class respectability.

Homage to Catalonia, Orwell's masterful account of serving on the side of the Loyalists in the Spanish Civil War, charts the disillusionment and danger that befell him as a member of the militia of a political party, the Party of Marxist Unification. His political education came to a crisis when he discovered in Spain that to achieve their aims the Communists would both murder their enemies (seeming to hate those on the left more than those on the right) and murder the past, in their willingness to rewrite it for political purposes.

Like the politicians I've been using as a counterpoint in this discussion, Orwell recognized the need for authority but also that it must be treated with some reserve, looked at carefully, as it was far too prone to take over the society that it was meant to protect, to transform itself into Big Brother. One should not be swallowed up by the establishment but preserve an independent critical stance; that was Orwell's determination. He had been trained to be a "responsible leader," but, like the politicians, he would not fit easily into that role; rather, he would redefine the role so that it would serve his own values of independence and imagination. Out of that experience came *Animal Farm* and *Nineteen Eighty-Four*, wherein he depicts the perversion of authority. After Spain he knew what he wanted: to turn society around and preserve what he saw as the abiding values of the England that he loved. At the end of *Homage to Catalonia*, he captured this feeling—along with a sense of the dangers that hovered over a free society such as the English enjoyed, in a world increasingly falling into totalitarianism. Returning from Spain, he writes in his final pages an elegy of love and grim prophecy for his native country:

And then England—southern England, probably the sleekest landscape in the world. . . . The industrial towns were far away, a smudge of smoke and misery hidden by the curve of the earth's surface. Down here it was still the England I had known in my childhood: the railway-cuttings smothered in wild flowers, the deep meadows where the great shining horses browse and meditate, the slow-moving streams bordered by willows, the green bosoms of the elms, the larkspurs in the cottage gardens; and then the huge peaceful wilderness of outer London, the barges on the miry river, the familiar streets, the posters telling of cricket matches and Royal weddings, the men in bowler hats, the pigeons in Trafalgar Square, the red buses, the blue policemen—all sleeping the deep, deep sleep of England, from which I sometimes fear that we shall never wake till we are jerked out of it by the roar of bombs.[10]

Much the same feeling imbues some famous lines in *The Lion and the Unicorn* that he is writing while "highly civilized human beings are flying overhead, trying to kill me." And he goes on:

England is not the jewelled isle of Shakespeare's much-quoted passage, nor is it the inferno depicted by Dr. Goebbels. More than either it resembles a family, a rather stuffy Victorian family, with not many black sheep in it but all its cupboards bursting with skeletons. It has rich relations who have to be kow-towed to and poor relations who are horribly sat upon, and there is a deep conspiracy of silence about the source of the family income. It is a family in which the young are generally thwarted and most of the power is in the hands of irresponsible uncles and bedridden aunts. Still, it is a family. It has its private language and its common memories, and at the approach of an enemy it closes its ranks. A family with the wrong members in control—that, perhaps, is as near as one can come to describing England in a phrase.[11]

Orwell undoubtedly would not have shared all the goals of the four political leaders I have mentioned. But he shared with them a feeling of strong support for their society, combined with a critical stance, a feeling of rebelliousness, and a conviction of a need for both a transformation of England as he knew it, and the need to preserve its standing values. The relationship of these maverick figures to their society was a complex one. They were using it—indeed almost exploiting it—for their own personal fulfillment. But their ultimate purpose was both to protect and enrich—despite Orwell's disclaimer—"this jewelled isle."

What, you may well ask, has this to do with *Nineteen Eighty-Four*? As an English historian, I think it useful to provide some context for the book, in particular the context of the author himself. *Nineteen Eighty-Four* quite rightly is taken to have general significance but, as Orwell himself stated, it is a blending of the traditional realist English novel with elements of fantasy. His original title for the book—"The Last Man in Europe"—is in fact much more accurate than the quirkily chosen date. But then if that first title had been retained, the phenomenon of so much attention being paid to the book would not have occurred—it would have been just a novel—and the power of its message would not have been as fully experienced.

Orwell was defending English values in his classic, negative, and perhaps overstated way in *Nineteen Eighty-Four*; doing so he was expressing his Englishness. The novel is concerned with three great competing powers in a vast world system. Yet it takes place mostly in London with a very brief visit to the countryside of Airstrip One for a love scene. Orwell believed in privacy—the privacy of personal life and the privacy of one's own thoughts. He believed in the great importance of the word and the protection of language for our intellectual freedom. He believed in the preservation of the past in its records and artifacts, such as an antique paperweight, or folksongs handed on through generations, the memories of ordinary people. He was a social historian before his time. He demonstrated the dangers of totalitarianisms of the left—and by implication, of the right—to these freedoms. He wished to achieve a state of democratic socialism that would preserve the values of his country, right or left. *Nineteen Eighty-Four* is not a great monument of literature, but in its depiction of a dehumanized world, it is a warning of what the future might bring if we allow Englishness—or Americanness—or any sort of individualness to wither away. Better a last living man in Europe than a horde of live-seeming robots, crying out, "We love Big Brother."

Notes

1. George Orwell, *Nineteen Eighty-Four*, 70th printing, (New York: New American Library, 1983), 5.
2. Peter Stansky and William Abrahams, *The Unknown Orwell* (New York: Knopf, 1972), 61.
3. Sonia Orwell and Ian Angus, eds., *The Collected Essays, Journalism and Letters of George Orwell*, 4 vols. (London: Secker & Warburg, 1968), 4:355-56.
4. Cyril Connolly, *Enemies of Promise*, rev. ed. (New York: Macmillan, 1948), 160.
5. Orwell, *Collected Essays*, 4:361.
6. Ibid., 1:540.
7. George Orwell, *The Lion and the Unicorn* (London: Secker & Warburg, 1941), 54-55.
8. George Orwell, *The Road to Wigan Pier* (London: Secker & Warburg, 1937), 149.
9. Orwell, *Collected Essays*, 1:240.
10. George Orwell, *Homage to Catalonia* (New York: Harcourt, Brace, 1952), 321-32.
11. Orwell, *Lion*, 34-35.

Discussion

The first questioner asked Mr. Stansky to compare the circumstances leading William Gladstone, Benjamin Disraeli, David Lloyd George, and Winston Churchill into political life with the circumstances of Orwell's career. Mr. STANSKY replied that his own concern in his lecture was with their social similarities, their attitudes toward English society, and their shared belief in change from within. The four were driven to become active politicians from the beginning, whereas Orwell was driven to be a writer, becoming intensely political in the last fourteen or fifteen years from *The Road to Wigan Pier* on. The lecture tried to show, in fruitful parallels with the four, that Orwell was more deeply rooted in his society than he has been given credit for.

An invitation from the floor to reflect on the role of women in Orwell's life and work stimulated considerable comment. Ms. CALDER's response was that the women who gave him support and companionship were significant; but that, had they not existed in his life, his output, his way of writing, thinking, and responding to the world around him, would not have been significantly different. She went on to say that his view of the traditional English working-class home pictured the man "sitting there reading the *Racing Times* . . . and the woman . . . doing her knitting . . . or sewing. . . . It would be very hard, I think, to find evidence of feminism in Orwell's writing." Mr. STANSKY observed that Orwell's attitude toward women was, in many ways, more traditional than that of Disraeli and Lloyd George. He noted that Daphne Patai, in her forthcoming "very interesting, very controversial, very misguided, very exciting" book *The Orwell Mystique: A Study in Male Ideology* (University of Massachusetts Press, 1984), gives Orwell an "extremely angry . . . feminist reading." In her book, Mr. STANSKY said, "she begins by saying that she worshipped Orwell, which I think is perhaps an unhealthy way to begin, and then she felt betrayed by him." Comments on Orwell's wife Eileen included Mr. STANSKY's that she supported his career, put herself second, served his needs, and made for "a satisfying, happy marriage"; and Mr. CRICK's that she would rough it, went to Spain, kept the accounts for the ILP (Independent Labour Party), "was as careless of her health as Orwell was careless of his health," but that "she did, in fact, neglect him in his eyes quite a lot, for the work she did for her brother." Adding a point about Orwell's writing, Mr. CRICK remarked that "he couldn't paint a female character on the page, except possibly Julia, who's a tough working-class girl: I think that's a very realistic portrait."

Lively discussion among Ms. CALDER, Messrs. STANSKY, CRICK, HECHT, and EDWARD WEISMILLER (from the floor) centered on Orwell's statement in his essay "Why I Write" (1946) that "all writers are vain, selfish and lazy." Ms. CALDER's position is that writers must be vain, "otherwise they wouldn't be writing"; that since writers must put writing before everything else, Orwell had to be selfish, but that his selfishness gave him such pangs that he "overcompensated for this tendency"; that while it is difficult to know what Orwell was getting at concerning laziness, he may have been suggesting that, for writers with a natural talent, writing is just doing what comes naturally, something of a self-indulgence, not real work. With laziness and Orwell, she, with others, finds a problem: "I doubt if there are many writers who, however naturally talented they are, would go along with that feeling about the business of writing." It was mentioned from the floor that, by "lazy," Orwell meant that writing is very difficult—most writers would rather not write; it is "just too hard, so they find ways of evading it. And it becomes harder," the comment went on, "once you have begun publishing, to match what you have done." Mr. HECHT brought up two poets who "fit the pattern perfectly": Byron and Frost. Both admitted they were vain and selfish, and Frost's particular slant on laziness was that writing was, "in some very special way, not productive of the welfare of human society in any easy, measurable way" commensurate with going out and holding a job as, for example, a policeman, a soldier, or a teacher. In Mr. STANSKY's view, the crucial phrase in the same essay is "being driven," because the driven writer feels that, no matter how much one has accomplished—"and certainly Orwell was fantastically productive"—one has not "done as much as [one] could or should." "I'd go further than that," Mr. CRICK added, "and say that [Orwell] was joking. He was an absolutely obsessive workaholic . . . and his friends and most of his readers all know that he was joking, surely." After an exchange between EDWARD WEISMILLER ("Every moment that you spent working against your will would convince you that you were lazy. Ask Tony [Hecht] if he doesn't think he's basically vain and selfish and lazy!") and Mr. HECHT ("I always think that."), a member of the audience speculated that Orwell "is saying that 'War is Peace and Laziness is Workaholic.' "

Ms. CALDER, asked from the floor to compare Arthur Koestler's *Darkness at Noon* with Orwell's writing, made four points. (1) Orwell, admiring Koestler tremendously and regretting the "boiled-rabbit" left-wing English intellectuals' insularity from what was going on in Europe, in contrast to Koestler's first-hand experiences, would have seen Koestler as "a stronger, tougher writer" than Orwell himself. (2) Whereas Koestler, however, was looking backward to the Russian purges, writing about something that *had* happened, Orwell (writing, nonetheless, "with Koestler's experience and what that represented very much in mind") focused on the life and society around him, in which he could see the germs of ominous possibilities. (3) A great difference between the two authors is that, while Orwell was English, Koestler was middle-European, writing *Darkness at Noon* in German, which was not his native language. From this difference between them stems another (4), that of style: Koestler, not writing in his own language, wrote with the enhanced precision characteristic of the writer who is "perhaps rather self-conscious about each word that [he is] choosing."

Eric Arthur Blair's pseudonym, "George Orwell," first used in *Down and Out in Paris and London* (1933), was the subject of some discussion between Mr. STANSKY and the audience. Mr. STANSKY believes that the most immediate reason Orwell wrote to his agent Leonard Moore of his desire to publish under a pseudonym was that Orwell "felt he might embarrass his family." Orwell's own suggested possible pseudonyms included "H. Lewis Allways" and "X," and he himself preferred "George Orwell." Once Orwell had written under the pseudonym, however, very complex psychological events followed, which Mr. STANSKY said "would require much too long to go into." Mr. STANSKY feels that the pseudonym was very important to Orwell and called it a parallel name to Winston Smith, in that "George" is the quintessence of Englishness, "Orwell" is a river in Suffolk, "Winston" stands for Churchill, and "Smith" for Everyman. In Orwell's surviving correspondence, his real name is used with family members and people he knew before the Spanish Civil War, and "George Orwell" with people he knew after Spain. On his tombstone "there is no mention of George Orwell." Mr. CRICK told of hearing recently from a correspondent that there was a race horse named "Orwell," "which came in last but one" in the first year the pseudonym was used. Mr. STANSKY commented that "P.S. Burton" was the name Orwell "used to tramp under." A member of the audience pointed out that both "Orwell" and "Allways" are close anagrams of (H. G.) Wells, a mentor of Orwell. Another comment from the floor, referring to George Woodcock's radio series called "Radio Biographies of Orwell," described the reminiscence in a January 1984 broadcast by a childhood friend (the friend identified by Mr. STANSKY as Mabel Fierz, and the story called "unlikely") that Orwell and his father were walking by the Orwell River before *Down and Out* came out and, after settling on "Orwell" for the surname, agreed on "George," his father's suggestion, for the first name—apparently a family joke, since "the father would frequently address strange boys as 'George.' "

A member of the audience, asking Ms. CALDER to elaborate on the origins of Orwell's commitment to the collective ideal and his subsequent rejection of it to become a "great champion of the individual against the tyranny of larger groups and organizations," recalled a passage from *Homage to Catalonia* in which Orwell, on leave in Barcelona, approves the camaraderie of the anarchists and finds "the true embodiment of the collective ideal." What about his rebellion against social and political groups? Ms. CALDER replied that, although the brief moment of collectivity that Orwell could identify with in the Spanish experience was "shattered in the most brutal fashion," the Spanish experience did not shatter his socialism—"far from it, I think it reinforced his socialism. In fact, his socialism really only took shape after that experience." She continued that his steering clear of any group or organization (except the Independent Labour Party) irritated his fellow socialists extraordinarily and laid him open to accusations of having turned away from socialism. When a member of the audience expressed surprised curiosity that such a product of a traditional background—family, Eton, the police, tight-knit groups—could become a rebel and associate with "this type of group to begin with," Ms. CALDER declared: "He believed that the world had to be changed, to put it in its simplest way. He believed that society was unequal, and that this was wrong, and that something should be done about it."

Mr. CRICK, from the floor, questioned the similarity between Mr. STANSKY's four prime ministers and Orwell ("I wonder if you were right to draw the analog of the four great leaders"), given Orwell's throwing himself in more with the politically contentious common man, the yeoman, the lower middle class, than with the establishment, and given that it was this alternative view—"the kind of thing that Michael Foot still shares to this day . . . and not the image of the great leaders"—that defined Orwell's patriotism. "The English socialist," Mr. CRICK maintained, "sees the analog of English socialism in the Civil War, in the American War of Independence, in Chartism"—this is Orwell's kind of patriotism.

Mr. STANSKY, in response, said "that sort of picture may well be a further similarity than a contradiction." It was Mr. STANSKY's position in making the analogy that Orwell's parallel to the four figures was specifically in his relationship with the ruling class and with authority. But they all—"certainly Disraeli, probably Churchill, perhaps Gladstone, perhaps Lloyd George"—would find this John Bull yeoman class the true Englishman, the heart of England.

Nineteen Eighty-Four:
The Book

Nineteen Eighty-Four: Politics and Fable

by Denis Donoghue

When we are speaking casually, we call *Nineteen Eighty-Four* a novel, but in a more exacting context we call it a political fable; political because it appears to deal with human life in society. This account of it is not refuted by the fact that we recall the book as preoccupied with an individual, Winston Smith, who suffers from a varicose ulcer, and that it takes account of other individuals, including Julia, Mr. Charrington, Mrs. Parsons, Syme, and O'Brien. These figures claim our attention, but they exist mainly in their relation to the political system that determines them. It would indeed be possible to think of them as figures in a novel, though in that case they would have to be imagined in a far more diverse set of relations. They would no longer inhabit or sustain a fable, because a fable is a narrative relieved of much contingent detail so that it may stand forth in an unusual degree of clarity and simplicity. What a fable says is that the world is essentially like this image of it, even though it has many other qualities which the image ignores. The fabulist's sense of life may be as responsive as anyone else's to contingency, the clash of chances and choices, but for the sake of his fable he sacrifices this sense to another one, his presentation of life chiefly as a *type* of life. A fable is a typology, a structure of types, each of them deliberately simplified lest a sense of difference and heterogeneity reduce the force of the typical. The claim a fabulist makes is that his narrative is essentially true; that the narrative truly represents the form and destiny of the world. Let us say, then, that *Nineteen Eighty-Four* is a political fable, projected into a near future in a mood variously to be described as one of threat, warning, despair, or rage, and incorporating historical references mainly to document a canceled past.

If a fable is predicated upon a typology, it is likely to be written as if from a certain distance. We recognize a type of person by abstracting certain features from many people, different in other respects, who share them. But we can't retain that sense of similarity while we immerse ourselves in detail and differentiation. A fable, in this respect, asks to be compared to a caricature, not to a photograph. It follows that in a political fable there is bound to be some tension between a political sense, which deals in the multiplicity of social and personal life, and a sense of fable, which is committed to simplicity of form and feature. If the political sense were to prevail, the narrative would be drawn away from fable into the novel, at some cost to its simplicity. If the sense of fable were to prevail, the fabulist would station himself at such a distance from any imaginary conditions in the case that his narrative would appear unmediated, free or bereft of conditions. The risk in that procedure would be considerable: a reader might feel that the fabulist has lost interest in the variety of human life and fallen back upon an unconditioned sense of its types, that he has become less interested in lives than in a particular idea of life. The risk is greater still if the fabulist projects his narrative into the future: the reader can't question it by appealing to the conditions of life he already knows. He is asked to believe that the future, too, like the past in *The Go-Between,* is another country, and that in all probability they do things differently there. In a powerful fable the reader's feeling is likely to be mostly fear: he is afraid that the fabulist's vision of any life that is likely to arise may be accurate and will be verified in the event. The fabulist's feeling may be more various. Such a fable as *Nineteen Eighty-Four* might arise from disgust, despair, or world-weariness induced by evidence that nothing, despite one's best efforts, has changed and that it is too late now to hope for the change one wants.

It is fairly generally agreed that Orwell's sense of the political fable as a genre was influenced, in various ways, by at least five examples of it: these, in chronological order, are *Gulliver's Travels* (1726), Jack London's *The Iron Heel* (1908), Yevgeny Zamyatin's *We* (written in 1920 and published in English translation in 1924), Huxley's *Brave New World* (1930), and Koestler's *Darkness at Noon* (1940). It is also agreed, but less generally, that *Nineteen Eighty-Four* was more immediately influenced by James Burnham's books, especially by *The Managerial Revolution,* which was published in England in May 1942. Burnham's books are discursive, not fictional; they are concerned to say how the world will be, not to show it in that character. But in any case the books I have listed are so different from one another that in bringing them together as political fables we have to take care not to sink their differences.

At the same time, the books have certain preoccupations in common. Each imagines a form of life ordained so completely in accordance with a particular set or model that the perfection of its character is monstrous. Any principle, enforced with impeccable logic, is monstrous, as Orwell recognized in *Nineteen Eighty-Four* by showing the good principle of communication carried to the mad pedantry of its conclusion, the vetoing of privacy. In each of these books, human beings who have come to value their uniqueness, their differences one from another, are forced to relinquish that conviction and to lapse into an undifferentiated state of being. In each book, history is shown as having ended by coinciding once for all with an imperative declaration of its meaning: existence has removed itself from historical process and culminated in an irresistible essence, withdrawing from every attribute but its official meaning.

Perfection, in the sense in which it is featured in these books, means the state of being complete, fully in accordance with the terms prescribed for it;

as a proposition in logic might be faultless, or a theorem in mathematics. The terms of the prescription might be those of biology and genetic engineering, as in *Brave New World;* or of mathematics and mechanical engineering, as in *We;* or of the technology of omnivorous communication, as in *Nineteen Eighty-Four*. Perfection, in any form, would be especially repugnant to Orwell, an English socialist who wanted for political life not a fixed principle but a decently mixed economy.

The plot of such a book would then suggest itself along a fairly obvious line. Suppose the perfection of a political system were endangered by some residual sentiments in one of its citizens; or, worse still, in two, who might be drawn together to make a little rival world. The perfection of the system would either be spoiled, or it would have to be enforced upon the deviant citizens. In the major political fables the plot shows the deviants perfectly assimilated to the system at the end. But there are many cosier fables, including a TV series some years ago called "The Prisoner," in which a determined and ingenious citizen maintains his selfhood and ties the system in knots.

Of the books I have mentioned, those which seem to have meant most to Orwell, whether he accepted their images or not, are *We* and *The Managerial Revolution*. So far as I know, Isaac Deutscher was the first to establish the bearing of *We* upon *Nineteen Eighty-Four,* and to show that Orwell's book to some extent draws upon Zamyatin's for its plot. In *We* the narrator, known only as D-503, works as an engineer in a society called The One State, a marvel in the engineering of glass. All goes perfectly until D-503 is roused to imperfection by a woman known as E-330. In the end, the system wins: D-503 is carried off to Auditorium 112, where he undergoes an operation and is reconciled to the perfection of rationality.[1] Orwell read the book in a French translation in February 1944: he started working on *Nineteen Eighty-Four* in 1945: he published a review of *We* in *Tribune* on January 4, 1946.[2] He finished *Nineteen Eighty-Four* in 1948. In the review he made the point that *Brave New World* was clearly based upon *We*. His own debt to *We* is mainly a matter of several affinities: Orwell's "Thought Police" are close to Zamyatin's "Guardians," his "Big Brother" is like Zamyatin's "Benefactor," and the particular form of imperfection is a love-affair. But the crucial consideration is that Zamyatin's book showed Orwell how he might move beyond the allegory of *Animal Farm*. In the review Orwell said that "what Zamyatin seems to be aiming at is not any particular country but the implied aims of industrial civilisation." To avoid repeating *Animal Farm*, Orwell had to find a larger or, better still, universal system of reference. Zamyatin showed him how it might be done, and how features of "the novel" could be drawn into "the fable." Many details in *Nineteen Eighty-Four* clearly refer to Russia. Big Brother has the ruggedly handsome face of Stalin, given not only historical but mythological status. Emmanuel Goldstein is clearly Trotsky. But the drabness of Oceania, the rationing of chocolate, the pervasive dreariness of the place testify to Orwell's dispirited sense of English life before, during, and immediately after the war. Much of this sentiment is drawn from the experience attributed to George Bowling in *Coming Up for Air,* the colorlessness of English working-class life despite whatever good could be said of it, and the guilt English intellectuals should bear for letting the workers sink into such drugged apathy. This part of *Nineteen Eighty-Four* also issues from the failure of Attlee's government to give English society any real vitality. More particularly, the Ministry of Truth, where Winston Smith works, comes from Orwell's experience of the British Ministry of Information during the war, and the lies purveyed in the evening news by the B.B.C.'s assurance, following bombing raids on German cities, that "all our aircraft returned home safely." The shifting alliances between the three powers, Oceania, Eurasia, and Eastasia, are based in the first instance on those between Russia and Germany, and, I think, on the postwar arrangements between the great powers as recorded in a famous photograph of Stalin, Roosevelt, and Churchill at Yalta.

Zamyatin's book showed Orwell that he could go beyond *Animal Farm* by moving freely between local reference and wider, more diffuse implication: the ideal form would be a series of short, brittle chapters illustrating various aspects of the system while discounting any possibility of a development within it. Each chapter would be an illustration, controlled by the idea governing the whole book. The form, like the system, would be entirely closed. Oceania lives only by repeating itself. The same applies, indeed, to any corporation—hence the fear provoked by a collectivity. Much of the power of *Nineteen Eighty-Four* arises from the reader's sense of a system which perpetuates itself without human intervention.

In practice, most political theorists have distinguished between three entities: the individual person, the society in which he lives, and the state. It is also normal to begin with the individual person and then to consider society as the embodiment of his nature as a social being, the relations he makes, his participation in personal and social experience. The state would then be a more distant entity, engaged in such matters as legislation, taxation, foreign relations, alliances, war, and peace. But suppose this division of purposes were to be perverted: suppose the state were to become an oligarchy so omnivorous that it swallowed up society and made the individual person a mere function of itself. That supposition is Orwell's vision, but it came to him nearly readymade, complete in every respect except a fictional form, from Burnham's books, and from three in particular, *The Managerial Revolution, The Machiavellians,* and *The Struggle for the World.*

Burnham changed his mind on points of detail, large and small, between one book and the next, mainly because—as Orwell pointed out—he thought that what was happening at each moment was decisive and that it would persist. But his general sense of the form political and administrative power would take didn't move far from the version of it he gave in *The Managerial Revolution.* In that book he predicted that the weakness of capitalism would continue to show itself; mainly because capitalism couldn't cope with mass unemployment, couldn't deal with public debts, or resuscitate a dying agriculture, couldn't handle its own resources, or do anything with an impotent bourgeois ideology. However, the downfall of capitalism would not mean the victory of the proletariat or any Marxist paradise. Capitalism would not be replaced by any form of socialism: autocracy was even more extreme in Stalin's Russia than in Hitler's Germany. This would not mean that states nominally socialist would revert to capitalism: instead, they would move toward a managerial form. Burnham's idea of managers was simple: they are the people who direct the process of production. A managerial state is based upon state ownership of the major instruments of production; more and more government control of the economy. Such a state would be the "property" not of rich men or capitalists but of managers: the managers would be the ruling class.

Burnham argued that the countries which had already gone furthest toward the managerial revolution were in fact the totalitarian dictatorships. What distinguished totalitarian dictatorship was "the number of facets of life subject to the impact of the dictatorial rule":

It is not merely political actions, in the narrower sense, that are involved; nearly every side of life, business and art and science and education and religion and recreation and morality are not merely influenced by but directly subjected to the totalitarian regime.[3]

But the managerial state, Burnham supposed, would be an oligarchy in possession of an exploiting economy. Managers would control the instruments of production in their own corporate favor: sovereignty would be located in various administrative bureaus which would displace parliament and issue decrees. An economy of state ownership would provide the basis for domination and exploitation "by a ruling class of an extremity and absoluteness never before known." The masses would be curbed or constantly diverted so that they would, as we say, go along with the managerial arrangements.

Zamyatin envisaged one world-state, but Burnham allowed for three. Three super-states would divide the world between them and would enter into shifting alliances with one another. In 1941 Burnham thought the three would be the United States, Europe (meaning Germany, the Netherlands, Belgium, northern France, and England), and "the Japanese islands together with parts of eastern China." The superpowers would wage war over marginal territory. "Ostensibly," Burnham said, "these wars will be directed from each base for conquest of the other bases. But it does not seem possible for any one of these to conquer the others; and even two of them in coalition could not win a decisive and lasting victory over the third." Or, as Orwell wrote in *Nineteen Eighty-Four*, "None of the three super-states could be definitively conquered even by the other two in combination."

Orwell published two important essays on Burnham in May 1946 and March 1947.[4] In the first, he gave a severe account of *The Managerial Revolution* and *The Machiavellians,* partly because several of Burnham's predictions had already been disproved. But Orwell was also irritated by Burnham's habit of thinking that because something was the case, it must continue to be the case. Orwell argued that "the real question is not whether the people who wipe their boots on us during the next fifty years are to be called managers, bureaucrats, or politicians: the question is whether capitalism, now obviously doomed, is to give way to oligarchy or to true democracy." He also maintained that Burnham, while attacking totalitarianism in all its forms and especially in its Russian form, was infatuated by its images: he was fascinated by the power he attacked and despised the democracy he should have defended. Indeed, Orwell accused Burnham of voicing the secret desire of the English intelligentsia, the desire "to destroy the old, equalitarian version of Socialism and usher in a hierarchical society where the intellectual can at last get his hands on the whip." At the end of the essay, Orwell offered his own prediction:

If I had to make a prophecy, I should say that a continuation of the Russian policies of the last fifteen years . . . can only lead to a war conducted with atomic bombs, which will make Hitler's invasion look like a tea-party. But at any rate, the Russian regime will either democratise itself, or it will perish. The huge, invincible, everlasting slave empire of which Burnham appears to dream will not be established, or, if established, will not endure, because slavery is no longer a stable basis for human society.

Nonetheless, in May 1946, Orwell found Burnham's general thesis of a managerial revolution plausible. A few months later he reviewed *The Struggle for the World:* by March 1947 America, but not Russia, had the atomic bomb. Burnham now took the view that the three superpowers envisaged in *The Managerial Revolution* were not, after all, morally much of a muchness. There were now, in any event, only two such powers, and one of them, the United States, was morally vastly superior to the other. Logic would suggest a preventive war against Russia, since Russia was clearly preparing to destroy the western democracies. At the very least, the United States should immediately draw Britain and as much of Europe as possible into an anti-Communist crusade.

Orwell's response to Burnham's arguments was fairly mild. He thought an anti-Communist crusade would probably come about, but he hoped that it might be possible to establish democratic socialism over an area of the globe as large as, say, western Europe and Africa. "If one could somewhere present the spectacle of economic security without concentration camps, the pretext for the Russian dictatorship would disappear and Communism would lose much of its appeal." If that were out of the question, then only two possibilities would remain. Russia might become more liberal and less dangerous over a period of a generation or so, if war could be avoided in the meantime. The other possibility, Orwell said, "is that the great powers will be simply too frightened of the effects of atomic weapons ever to make use of them." In either case, Orwell cheered himself up by thinking that history would not be as melodramatic as Burnham's predictions.

But it is clear that while Orwell rejected many of Burnham's arguments, he found the plot and indeed some of the imagery of *The Managerial Revolution* highly persuasive. The book was a good description, he said in 1947, of "what is actually happening in various parts of the world, i.e. the growth of societies neither capitalist nor Socialist, and organised more or less on the lines of a caste system." He couldn't refute Burnham's arguments; all he could do was find them distastefully extreme and hope for a political future somewhat quieter and more tolerant than anything Burnham envisaged. He wanted a world in which states would indeed exist, but in which decent societies would be allowed to thrive. The source of his most acute anxiety in *Nineteen Eighty-Four* is the fate of self, individuality, and mind in a system that reduces them to mere repetitions of the same. What he most fears in the technology of communication is the loss of privacy, the fact that O'Brien knows what Winston Smith is thinking even before Smith has articulated it for himself. "They can't get inside you," Julia said. "But they could get inside you," Winston learns. Orwell rebuked Burnham for not asking himself what power is for: power to do what? But in *Nineteen Eighty-Four* power is for the sake of power. Winston and Julia are forced to betray each other because the Party wants to exercise its power.

Nineteen Eighty-Four doesn't even try to refute Burnham on his own terms: it doesn't offer the world a more accommodating destiny. But it shifts the terms of discourse to discourse itself: the fate of the world is to be represented by analogy with the fate of language, and specifically of the English language. The main reason for this shift is that while it is reasonable to feel that the English language is being corrupted, it is also reasonable to feel—what few of us can claim in politics—that we can still take action to save it.

I have mentioned Orwell's experience of the B.B.C. and the Ministry of Information during the war. I think he felt misgiving, at least, about the daily work of propaganda, even in a cause he believed to be just. In an essay, "Writers and Leviathan," which he wrote in March 1948, he distinguished between the citizen and the writer: when they are one and the same person, the citizen should do nearly any work for his political party, but he should not write for it or engage in propaganda in its behalf. A man's work for a cause should be the rough-and-ready thing it usually is, but his writings should always be "the product of the saner self that stands aside, records the things that are done and admits their necessity, but refuses to be deceived as to their true nature." I think Orwell also felt that this saner self was particularly available to an Englishman because of the splendor of the English language. He felt that English, if we treat it decently, is an instrument of unique capacity. Indeed, he shared this sentiment with men as different in other respects as Herbert Read, Robert Graves, and—his colleague in wartime propaganda—William Empson. Empson has an early essay in which he maintains that a decent English style "gives great resilience to the thinker, never blurs a point by too wide a focus, is itself a confession of how much always must be left undealt with, and is beautifully free from verbiage. To an enemy it looks like sheer cheating." Empson's *The Structure of Complex Words*, Herbert Read's *English Prose Style*, and Graves's book, written with Alan Hodge, *The Reader over Your Shoulder* issue from much the same experience as Orwell's essay "Politics and the English Language."

"Politics and the English Language" is closer to the interests of *Nineteen Eighty-Four* than to anything else Orwell wrote: it is the essay to read when the theme is his ideology of "the plain style" and the political attitudes it supports. Orwell's sense of language could not have been simpler. He was indifferent to philosophical issues, and most of all to issues in the philosophy of language. He would certainly have despised our current preoccupation with questions of indeterminacy, logocentrism, and the like. He regarded a language—the English language, for instance—as an instrument in the furtherance of thought. If the instrument is in good order, the mind can work well with it: if it is blunt, sloppy, or otherwise decayed, the mind is disabled. The English language, he said, "becomes ugly and inaccurate because our thoughts are foolish, but the slovenliness of our language makes it easier for us to have foolish thoughts." If thought corrupts language, "language can also corrupt thought." A writer writes well when he picks out words for the sake of their meaning and invents images to make his meaning clearer. Orwell also assumed that we can do our thinking without recourse to words, and that we go to words only to convey our meaning: he didn't advert to the notion that our thinking is already inscribed in the language native to us, and may be partly determined by its syntax.

The passage in "Politics and the English Language"[5] which makes Orwell's position entirely clear is this one:

What is above all needed is to let the meaning choose the word, and not the other way about. In prose, the worst thing one can do with words is to surrender to them. When you think of a concrete object, you think wordlessly, and then, if you want to describe the thing you have been visualising, you probably hunt about till you find the exact words that seem to fit it. When you think of something abstract you are more inclined to use words from the start, and unless you make a conscious effort to prevent it, the existing dialect will come rushing in and do the job for you, at the expense of blurring or even changing your meaning. Probably it is better to put off using words as long as possible and get one's meaning as clear as one can through pictures or sensations. Afterwards one can choose—not simply accept—the phrases that will best cover the meaning, and then switch round and decide what impression one's words are likely to make on another person.

Virtually every sentence in that passage is questionable: but that doesn't mean that it's demonstrably wrong. Most philosophers of language would maintain that the relation between mind and language is far more complex than Orwell implies. To what extent wordless thinking is possible is also a contentious matter. It is not clear what would be entailed in "letting the meaning choose the words": the phrase is culpably vague, since the meaning doesn't choose anything, it is the mind that chooses. Orwell's linguistics doesn't amount to more than the assertion that a pudding is a pudding, and that good plain cooking is the best.

But the aspect of the passage I want to look at more closely is its assumption that good plain writing is an ethical choice. Orwell believed that a writer who tries to write well takes the language—the English language, if that is the case—as the custodian of his best and sanest self. Part of the writer's concern is to rid himself of dying metaphors, pretentious diction, meaningless expressions. Another part is his effort to think of vivid images to make his meaning clearer. Now these concerns correspond, I think, to a writer's scruple: a good sentence issues from one's best self and from a language responsive to ethical choices. The effort of writing well is the writer's version of conscientiousness: a decent English prose is decent in an ethical sense, too, and not because it observes any official form of decorum.

Orwell doesn't say precisely how a language exerts this ethical authority. It doesn't, indeed, unless we let it. But *Nineteen Eighty-Four* makes it clear that the ethical authority of a language comes not only from the fact that we can say of some sentences that they are decent and of other sentences that they are corrupt: it comes more specifically, I think, from the history of the words in a language and from our respect for that history. The sense of the past is most acute in Orwell when it appears as respect for the associations of words; not casual or impressionistic associations but those which tell of all they have come through, their historical weight and density. Newspeak is the linguistic form of brainwashing. It is worth mentioning, too, that Empson's *The Structure of Complex Words* is based on the assumption that most of our feeling and sentiment is located in certain rich adhering words. Newspeak nullifies this accretion of feeling by disengaging words from their history; it is mostly a matter of abbreviating them. As Orwell says in the appendix to *Nineteen Eighty-Four*, "it was perceived that in thus abbreviating a name one narrowed and subtly altered its meaning, by cutting out most of the associations that would otherwise cling to it."[6] The words *Communist International*, for instance, "call up a composite picture of universal human brotherhood, red flags, barricades, Karl Marx, and the Paris Commune." But the word *Comintern* "suggests merely a tightly-knit organization and a well-defined body of doctrine." *Comintern* "is a word that can be uttered almost without taking thought, whereas Communist International is a phrase over which one is obliged to linger at least momentarily." What Orwell means by that lingering is one's response not only to the immediate meaning of a word but to the historical and moral experience it enacts. Newspeak, incidentally, may also have issued from Orwell's misgiving about such artifices as Esperanto and the Basic English of C.K. Ogden and I.A. Richards—products of good intention but, like "universal education," a far poorer thing in event and consequence than in anticipation.

It follows that two major concerns in *Nineteen Eighty-Four* are so close as to be nearly one: the mutability of history and the elimination, in Newspeak, of heretical words and the sentiments they embody. Orwell's understanding of history is nearly as unquestioning as his sense of language. He did not confront, as in our own time, the widespread disaffection from history and skepticism about historical knowledge. Orwell took it for granted that historical events were recoverable and that a decent, scrupulous mind, by taking thought, could make sense of them and offer that sense as their meaning. The mutability of history, in *Nineteen Eighty-Four*, is an outrage to Orwell because it mocks the efforts men have made to produce from historical events a privileged meaning; privileged in the sense of being self-evidently cogent and persuasive. In Oceania, the past, too, can be brainwashed.

I have been maintaining that Orwell's distinctive intervention in the tradition of the political fable was his representation of systematic cruelty and intimidation by analogy with the deliberate degradation of language. The fact that politics and language are both systems made the analogy available. But the most questionable aspect of the analogy is Orwell's implication, in both *Nineteen Eighty-Four* and "Politics and the English Language," that a decent style, specifically his own plain style, is directly sanctioned by nature. He doesn't acknowledge that writing in a plain style is just as much a rhetorical act as writing in, say, the style of Walter Pater or Sir Thomas Browne. No style arrives with the authority of nature. Orwell's plain style is not independent of rhetoric: indeed, only by a strikingly elaborate rhetoric was it possible to imply a "natural" kinship between his plain style, the truth of commonsense, a politics of decency, and a notion of historical truth as self-evident. Orwell contrived to enforce the assumption that his intimacy with these values was a matter of sound instincts and that rival values were merely forms of decadence issuing from a perverse intelligentsia. Such decadence was available to intellectuals because they weren't required to carry their notions into social and political practice.

The main problem in reading *Nineteen Eighty-Four* in 1984 is that the book has so often been compromised: it has rarely been read in a disinterested spirit or, as we say, as a work of literature. Like *Animal Farm*, it has been received by readers on the political right as irrefutable evidence that they have been accurate from the start in their judgment of Communism. The evidence has been particularly welcome, coming from a man who had good reason to know the character of Communism: he had seen such men, after all, in Spain. So *Nineteen Eighty-Four* has had far greater political reverberation than, say, Constantine Fitzgibbon's *When the Kissing Had to Stop*, because Fitzgibbon was never anything but a man of the right. *Animal Farm* and *Nineteen Eighty-Four* have been read as tracts for the times, especially by readers who practice a rhetoric of the Cold War, McCarthyism, or the version of those sentiments which is in some vogue again.

Readers whose political attitudes coincide with liberal democracy—or whose attitudes have changed to that position—have welcomed the book as a truthful indictment of totalitarianism. I am thinking of Philip Rahv, Irving Howe, and—in his general sense of Orwell's achievement—Lionel Trilling. Trilling's essay on *Homage to Catalonia* has been extremely influential in maintaining the impression that Orwell, by being a virtuous man, was what an evil time most urgently needed. Trilling's sense of Orwell is totally free from the triumphalism of the right—he doesn't produce Orwell's evidence with a flourish as if to say, "I told you so." But his essay has had one regrettable effect: it has established too firmly the kinship between Orwell's being a virtuous man and his endorsement of a certain set of attitudes. As a result, readers on the left have reacted, more strongly than they might otherwise have done, against the identification of virtue with the opinions Orwell held.

I am thinking of two such reactions. Isaac Deutscher's essay—which I have already mentioned—accused Orwell of indulging himself in the mysticism of cruelty. Having lost confidence in the power of intelligence, Orwell "increasingly viewed reality through the dark glasses of a quasi-mystical pessimism." Deutscher's charge against Orwell is the same as Orwell's against Burnham; that in the end, finding that plain open-air thinking hadn't transformed the world, he abandoned it in favor of fanaticism and hysteria. *Nineteen Eighty-Four*, according to Deutscher, has frightened millions of people, "but it has not helped them to see more clearly the issues with which the world is grappling. . . . it has only increased and intensified the waves of panic and hate that run through the world and obfuscate innocent minds."[7]

The second critic on the left I want to invoke is Raymond Williams. A socialist with occasional connections of discourse with Communists, Williams has often written about Orwell, sometimes with reluctant sympathy and respect, as in his "Modern Masters" book on him. But he now finds Orwell's books intolerable. In *Politics and Letters* (1979) he discussed Orwell with the editors of the *New Left Review*, who were hostile to Orwell in every particular. They asserted that: (1) Orwell didn't produce any new theoretical knowledge about society or history, and "*1984* will be a curio in 1984"; (2) his novels "range from the mediocre to the weak"; (3) his social reporting, as in *The Road to Wigan Pier*, is vitiated by suppression and manipulation of the evidence; (4) in the creation of a character called "Orwell," he indulged himself in masquerade "in the sense that under the guise of frankness and directness the writing posture is more than usually dominative." Williams didn't disagree with these views. In fact, he attacked the Orwell of *Nineteen Eighty-Four* in far more extreme terms. "The recruitment of very private feelings against socialism becomes intolerable," he said, "by *1984*":

> It is profoundly offensive to state as a general truth, as Orwell does, that people will always betray each other. If human beings are like that, what could be the meaning of a democratic socialism? . . . *Animal Farm*, for all its weaknesses, still makes a point about how power can be lost and how people can be misled: it is defeatist, but it makes certain pointed observations on the procedures of deception. As for *1984*, its projections of ugli-

ness and hatred, often quite arbitrarily and inconsequentially, onto the difficulties of revolution or political change seem to introduce a period of really decadent bourgeois writing in which the whole status of human beings is reduced.[8]

Williams accuses Orwell of capturing the role of the "frank, disinterested observer who is simply telling the truth," and then of producing as the truth a report entirely defeatist. I don't agree with Williams in this charge, but I understand his irritation—not to represent it as more than that—when he is asked, by Trilling, Howe, Kazin, and many other liberal writers, to revere Orwell as a virtuous and truth-telling man. It's like being asked to take Gandhi as a saint. In private life, Orwell seems to have been a decent man, but there is evidence of shoddy sentiments, and intermittently of cruel behavior to rather vulnerable people. The answer to this is that he deeply regretted his offences and, when they were public acts, confessed them, as in *Burmese Days*. But I don't think he was, in fact, a particularly nice man or that a halo sits well on his head. I'm sure he tried to tell the truth as he saw it and worried a great deal when he didn't tell it. But so do most people, even when in retrospect it emerges that they deceived themselves or fell into bewilderments they could have avoided.

But Williams's account of *Nineteen Eighty-Four* is not valid. The book doesn't say that people will always betray each other: you could derive that grim moral from it only if you claimed that you, for instance, would hold out forever against the most appalling torture; or that you, unlike hundreds of tortured people, could never be brainwashed. Again, Williams is inaccurate when he refers to Orwell's "extreme distaste for humanity of every kind, especially concentrated in figures of the working class." The only incident I can think of, in *Nineteen Eighty-Four*, as at all supporting that charge is the appalling fight of the two prole women over the saucepan—in many ways the most dreadful episode in the book. But in *Nineteen Eighty-Four* as a whole the proles get a better showing than anyone else; it is not their fault that they are kept in cultural sedation, like the English working-class, kept inert on drink, gambling, and the popular newspapers. But no such argument would satisfy Williams, short of representing the working class as ready and determined to fulfill the redemptive destiny Marx prescribed for them. Orwell's relation to the working class was indeed ambivalent: his sympathy was too much an act of goodwill to be really convincing. But he wasn't, after all, a member of the working class, so it is hardly surprising or scandalous that, while making every effort to like workers, he found them extremely limited in their interests and values.

A valid reading of *Nineteen Eighty-Four* would entail several recognitions. The book is not a documentary account of any regime; it is a fable, written in fear by a writer beset with his own illness and the illness of the world. I think Orwell was English in the sense we associate with Hardy and Elgar: the idyllic episode in *Nineteen Eighty-Four* evokes the English countryside in those terms. Experience of war and time of war—Barcelona and London—exasperated Orwell's sensibility to the point of making him, intermittently, conspire with what he feared and hated. He lent his imagination, I believe, to images and visions which did not endorse his discursive habit. Indeed, I think well of G.S. Fraser's view, outlined in a letter to *Critical Quarterly* in 1959, that *Nineteen Eighty-Four* is horrible because Orwell started to write it to say "this *may* happen," but his imagination turned that moral impulse into one of morose delectation, as if to say "this *must* happen." I think *Nineteen Eighty-Four* should be read much as the fourth book of *Gulliver's Travels* is read, though Orwell's imagination is of a much inferior power to Swift's. Both books have many local references, political allusions which only the elect recognize, but beyond these allusions both are universalist in their ambition, exempting no one from their strictures. What *Nineteen Eighty-Four* describes is a system. Orwell does not explain how the system came into being, unless we are to suppose one dreadful cause, the failure and treason of intellectuals. As it stands, the system is there; it is what it is; it corresponds to the exercise of power for the sake of power. René Girard has complained that the book does not show the connection between individual desire and the collective structure: "we sometimes get the impression from Orwell's books that the 'system' has been imposed from the outside on the innocent masses."[9] But that impression is consistent with the managerial character of the system; it is an oligarchy, and it has separated its activities from the proles. But I would make more than Girard does of the doubleness he speaks of in the totalitarian structure; especially as it is given in the relation between Winston Smith and O'Brien—which is not adequately thought of as one between a victim and his assailant. What is peculiarly insistent is the degree to which Winston feels himself drawn to speak to O'Brien and enters into extraordinary complicity with him: so far as the reader's access to it is in question, it is the most telling relation in the book. It is also the relation which underlines most compellingly the character and force of a system; its appalling capacity to operate independently of the people who compose it.

Notes

1. Yevgeny Zamyatin, *We*, trans. Bernard Guilbert Guerney (Harmondsworth: Penguin Books, 1972).
2. Sonia Orwell and Ian Angus, eds., *The Collected Essays, Journalism and Letters of George Orwell*, 4 vols. (London: Secker and Warburg, 1968), 4:75.
3. James Burnham, *The Managerial Revolution: Or What Is Happening in the World Now* (London: Putnam, 1942), 145.
4. Both essays are reprinted in vol. 4 of *The Collected Essays, In Front of Your Nose*, 160-81 and 313-25.
5. *The Collected Essays*, vol. 4, *In Front of Your Nose*, 127-39.
6. George Orwell, *1984* (Harmondsworth: Penguin Books, 1983), 264.
7. Isaac Deutscher, "*1984*: The Mysticism of Cruelty," in *Heretics and Renegades* (London: Hamish Hamilton, 1956); reprinted in Raymond Williams, ed., *George Orwell: A Collection of Critical Essays* (Englewood Cliffs, New Jersey: Prentice-Hall, 1974), 132.
8. Raymond Williams, *Politics and Letters* (London: NLB, 1979), 384-92.
9. René Girard, *Deceit, Desire, and the Novel*, trans. Yvonne Freccero (Baltimore and London: Johns Hopkins University Press, 1965), 226.

"NOT ONE OF US":
George Orwell and
Nineteen Eighty-Four

by Alfred Kazin

His subject matter will be determined by the age he lives in—at least this is true in tumultuous, revolutionary ages like our own—but before he ever begins to write he will have acquired an emotional attitude from which he will never completely escape.

George Orwell "Why I Write" (1946)

The system of organized lying on which society is founded.

Outline for *Nineteen Eighty-Four* (1943)

"Not one of us," snapped the Labour Party secretary in Limehouse. I was a reporter in wartime England interviewing him on Labour's plans for the postwar society and had asked him what he thought of George Orwell, a name then better known to Americans on the anti-Stalinist left than to most English and American readers before *Animal Farm* and *Nineteen Eighty-Four* made him world famous. Orwell had been writing the "London Letter" for *Partisan Review*, and he had written in *Homage to Catalonia* (1938) what I fondly thought of as *our* version of the Spanish Civil War: homage indeed to the Spanish Anarchists and to the proscribed P.O.U.M. in which Orwell had served, with other unaffiliated British radicals sympathetic to the Independent Labour Party; unyielding bitterness about the Stalinist apparatus in Spain that had helped give victory to Franco by its frustration of the spontaneous Spanish revolution and by its attempt to kill opposition on the left.

To the solid trade union official representing Labour in Limehouse, George Orwell the novelist and book critic, a columnist for Aneurin Bevan's left-wing *Tribune*, was just an intellectual and perhaps a class enemy as well. Without having read his books, the official knew that Orwell was an old Etonian and had gone to Burma as a member of the Indian Imperial Police. It was bitter winter, early 1945. Allied forces had not yet crossed the Rhine. The reconstruction of society that I heard so much of in British Army discussion groups—morale after Dunkirk was so low that the War Office, in a phrase inconceivable to Americans, announced, "We are going left with the troops," and had instituted the Army Bureau of Current Affairs, hard-hitting discussions officially part of the weekly routine—of course depended on the defeat of Hitler and in the postwar elections a Labour victory that seemed unthinkable in the face of Churchill's dominance. "Let Us Face The Future" was the title of Labour's program in the 1945 elections. A common regret of the period: "If only Churchill were Labour!" Well, he wasn't. Even as winter yielded to the glorious spring of 1945 and the first Michaelmas daisies sprouting in the bombed damp earth were pictured for morale posters reading "Renascence," much of the grime, violence, and deadly fatigue that were to go into *Nineteen Eighty-Four* remained all too familiar on the streets of wartime London.

In Orwell's novel thirty rocket bombs a week are falling on the capital; nothing more is said of them. Like the "atom bomb" in the novel that exploded over Oceania's "Airstrip One"—England—and by destroying a church provided a hiding place in the belfry for the lovers in an "almost deserted stretch of country," all these bombs are abstractions in a book that, except for the hardships of daily living borrowed from the 1940s, is meant to be an abstract of a wholly *political* future. Orwell was an efficient novelist not particularly interested in fiction; he used it for making a point. Bombs in *Nineteen Eighty-Four* symbolize Orwell's pent-up rage about everything in the political world from the mass unemployment of the 1930s (which continued well into the war period) to the ignorance of the left intelligentsia justifying Stalinism because the Russian people were pouring out their blood. By 1948, when Orwell was finishing up the novel he had conceived in 1943, he was also maddened by the postwar division of the world, the atom bombs on Japan, and England's dependency on America. The ex-radical neo-conservative proponents of America-as-ideology now trying to claim Orwell overlook the fact that England's currency in *Nineteen Eighty-Four* is American. England is Oceania Airstrip I. We know whose airstrip it is.

Winston Smith and his fellows in the Ministry Of Truth spend their days rewriting the past. But "Most of the material you were dealing with had no connection with anything in the real world, not even the kind of connection that is contained in a direct lie." Not Orwell's novel is fiction but the world itself. Fiction as deliberate abstraction from life is what this terror society lives on. By political fiction Orwell means a society that has no meaning. A collectivized insanity is what a wholly tendentious politics has reduced us to. *We* have become the vacuum. Appearance has replaced reality, and appearance is just propaganda. In this future emptiness any two of the three great powers dividing the world (Orwell was grimly sure there would soon be two) may be officially but only symbolically at war. This is a war without end, because it is probably being waged in the Ministry of Peace. Or if it is really going on, like the present war between Iran and Iraq, the belligerents have forgotten why they went to war. Truckloads of enemy prisoners are regularly shown to London, but they may not be prisoners or even enemies. Bombs do occasionally fall on the city, but like Somoza or Assad, the rulers of this society probably bomb their own people to keep them cowed.

By V-E Day over ten thousand rocket bombs had fallen on Britain; it would have been knocked out of the war if the enemy's bases had not been captured in time. The *thirty* bombs falling each week in *Nineteen Eighty-Four* are symbols of the routine terror that Orwell imagined for the end of the century. Politics for him had become the future as total domination. Total injustice had certainly become his vision of things. In *Nineteen Eighty-Four* only the total disregard of the masses by the Party (a theme fundamental to the book but not demonstrated as fully as the devastation of language and the elimination of the past) shows Orwell's compassion struggling against his shuddering vision of the future. "Work and bed," I used to hear English factory workers complain. "Might as well be dead." The deadly fatigue of 1939–45 is captured in one line about Winston Smith's neighbor Mrs. Parsons. "One had the impression that there was dust in the creases of her face."

What Orwell would not transfer from 1945 to 1984 were the positive and liberating aspects of wartime controls. England was in many respects more fully mobilized for war than Nazi Germany. There was a general improvement in national health and social services that convinced many people that such efficiency called for widespread nationalization. An impatient drive for a better life increasingly filled the atmosphere as Germany finally went down to defeat. To the amazement of many people in the "movement," this brought the Labour Party to power with the greatest majority in the history of British socialism. Orwell's writings of the period reflect little of this. It is true that he was ailing with the lung disease that was to kill him in 1950, that his wife Eileen had died in March 1945 when he was in Germany as a correspondent, that he was still writing for the left-wing *Tribune*, that the author of that wickedly brilliant satire on Stalinism, *Animal Farm*, continued to proclaim himself a supporter of the Labour Party and a libertarian socialist.

Nevertheless, the bread-and-butter issues that brought Labour to power did not get into the novel that made Orwell's name a symbol for the fear of socialism. The tyranny in his book is called "Ingsoc," English socialism. Like so many Americans on the left, Orwell was more concerned with what Russia portended for socialism than with the actual struggles of the working class. "Socialism" in America is just a rumpus between the nostalgic and ex-radicals. In England it was a national movement, a government in power, an aroused consciousness. What was more on Orwell's mind, despite his undiminished sympathy for Labour, was the issue of domination that he knew so well from his upper-class background, though he derived, he said, from the lower part of it. Or as Lenin put it, Who Whom?—who's going to run the show and drive the rest of us?

Socialism to George Orwell, as to the utopian reformers and idealists of the nineteenth century, was not an economic question but a moral one. The welfare state little interested Orwell. He was naive, or perhaps just literary, when he wrote in *The Road to Wigan Pier*, his documentary of British poverty in the thirties, "economic injustice will stop the moment we want it to stop, and no sooner, and if we genuinely want it to stop the method adopted hardly matters." To the twenty-six-year-old Karl Marx writing in the *Economic and Philosophical Manuscripts* (1844), the purpose of socialism was to end, for once in human history, the economic struggle for existence that has always kept man from "reappropriating" his essence. Exactly a century later Orwell wrote in a book review, "The real problem of our time is to restore the sense of absolute right and wrong when the belief that it used to rest on—that is, the belief in personal immortality—has been destroyed. This demands faith, which is a different thing from credulity."

Exactly at the moment when twentieth-century technology had shown itself capable of feeding the hungry, when everything in sight justified Marx's tribute in *The Communist Manifesto* to the new productive forces and Whitehead's praise of "the century of hope" for "inventing invention," socialism in its original meaning—the end of tribal nationalism, of man's alienation from his own essence, of wealth determining all values in society—yielded to the nightmare of coercion. What drove Orwell into opposition all his own, what made for the ominousness of *Nineteen Eighty-Four*, for a deadliness of spirit that fills the book and that helped to kill him at forty-six, was his inability to overlook the source of the nightmare. Lenin had seized the state in the name of the long-suffering working class. Thomas Hobbes in 1651 had called Leviathan "the mortal God." He ascribed its power over men to their fear of violent death at each other's hands in the brute state of nature. Fear causes men to create a state by contracting to surrender their natural rights and to submit to the absolute authority of a sovereign. By the social contract men had surrendered their natural liberties in order to enjoy the order and safety of the organized state. But under the total domination of the socialist state, men could be just as afraid of violent death at each other's hands as they had been in the state of nature.

"Socialism" was not a fetish to Orwell. He would not have been as contemptuous of social democracy as Arthur Koestler, who mocked Clement Attlee saying to the great crowd cheering his Party's astonishing victory in July 1945, "Don't expect too much of us. We're batting on a very sticky wicket." Orwell was repelled but fascinated by the progress of James Burnham from extreme left to extreme right. With his dislike of absolutist intellectuals, he would not have been astonished to see the ease with which so many ex-radicals have managed to overcome their disillusionment in the arms of the Pentagon, the C.I.A., the National Security Administration, and other current examples of how to get "the State off our backs." No great admirer of the United States, which he never cared to visit, Orwell would have made note of the fact that last year the average American household watched television for seven hours and two minutes each day, that households with cable now watch fifty-eight hours a week, and that in this year of 1984 readers of a liberal weekly could read the following:

Is Big Brother watching? If you are tired of Gov't . . . tired of Big Business . . . tired of everybody telling you who you are and what you should be . . . then now is the time to speak out . . . Display yr disgust and declare your independence . . . Wear a Big Brother Is Watching Shirt today, Tee shirt $10 / . . . Canadians remit $US. Big Brother Is Watching LTD, Neenah WI.

Orwell thought that the problem of domination by class or caste or race or political machine more atrocious than ever. It demands solution. Because he *was* upper-class and knew from his own prejudices just how unreal the lower classes can be to upper-class radicals, a central theme in all his work is the separateness and loneliness of the upper-class observer, like his beloved Swift among the oppressed Irish. We all know that he was born in India, that he was brought up to the gentility, snobbery, and race-pride of the British upper classes, especially in the more anxious forms of class consciousness dictated by genteel poverty. He was put through the scholarship mill for Eton and revolted against the system by not going on to Oxford or Cambridge, choosing instead to become a policeman in Burma. After five years of this, furiously rejecting British imperialism, he threw himself into the ranks of the *Lumpenproletariat* in Paris and London, the "people of the abyss," as his admired Jack London put it. In England he lived the life of a tramp for months at a time despite his weak lungs and after publishing his first book, *Down and Out in Paris and London* (1933), went out to the mining districts in the North to do his extraordinary first-hand investigation of working class life and poverty, *The Road to Wigan Pier* (1937).

Hostile critics of *Nineteen Eighty-Four* have eagerly picked on the fact that despite his attempt to immerse himself in working class life, Orwell did not commit himself to socialism until he returned to England in 1937 after being wounded in the Spanish Civil War and hunted by Loyalist police for having fought with the proscribed anti-Stalinist P.O.U.M. It was the wonderful fraternalism of the Anarchists and other anachronistic idealists on the left that gave Orwell his one image of socialism as a transformation of human relationships. In Catalonia, for a brief season after Franco's revolt in 1936, the word *Comrade* really meant something. In *Homage to Catalonia* Orwell recited with wonder the disappearance of the usual servility and money worship. What a glorious period that was—until the nominally socialist government in Madrid, instigated by the Communists, frustrated every possibility of social revolution from within. Even before Franco conquered in 1939, the old way of life had been restored in Catalonia.

Orwell never forgot what he had seen in Catalonia. This was more than "socialism with a human face," that desperate slogan of the doomed Czechs in 1968, it was socialism as true and passionate equality. Socialism, he wrote near the end of his life, can mean nothing but justice and liberty. For Orwell socialism was never a fetish, the sacred name now justifying one hideous tyranny after another, but the only possible terminus—where? when?—to the endless deprivations suffered by most human beings on earth. But since he equally abominated the despotisms still justified by many English and American left intellectuals, he made a point in *Nineteen Eighty-Four* of locating the evil in the thinking of the leading Thought Policeman, O'Brien.

Political intellectuals on the left, the ex-left, the would-be left, the ideological right, can be poison. By the time he summed up all his frustration and rage in *Nineteen Eighty-Four*, Orwell had gone beyond his usual contempt for what he called "the boiled rabbits of the left." He was obsessed by the kind of rationale created by modern intellectuals for tyranny by state. O'Brien's speeches to the broken Winston Smith in the Thought Police's torture chamber represent for Orwell the essence of our century's political hideousness. Although O'Brien says that power seeks power and needs no ideological excuse, he does in fact explain to his victim *what* this power is.

The power exerted and sought by political intellectuals is that they must always be right. O'Brien is frightening because of the way he thinks, not because of the cynicism he advances. Dostoevsky in *The Possessed* said of one of his revolutionist "devils"—"When he was excited he preferred to risk anything rather than to remain in uncertainty." O'Brien to his victim: "You are a flaw in the pattern, Winston. You are a stain that must be wiped out. . . . It is intolerable to us that an erroneous thought should exist anywhere in the world, however secret and powerless it may be."

Every despotism justifies itself by claiming the power of salvation. Before salvation by the perfect society, there was salvation by the perfect God. One faction after another in history represents perfection, to the immediate peril of those who do not. My salvation cannot tolerate your disbelief, for that is a threat to my salvation.

The key issue for which O'Brien tortures Winston Smith is O'Brien's necessary belief that the mind controls all things. There is in fact no external reality. The world is nothing but man and man nothing but mind. Winston, not yet electroshocked into agreeing to this, protests from his rack: "the world itself is only a speck of dust. And man is tiny—helpless! How long has he been in existence? For millions of years the earth was uninhabited." O'Brien: "Nonsense. The earth is as old as we are, no older. How could it be older? Nothing exists except through human consciousness. . . . Before man there was nothing. After man, if he could come to an end, there would be nothing. Outside man there is nothing."

That is the enemy in *Nineteen Eighty-Four*, and against it an exhausted and dying English radical, in the great tradition of English commonsense empiricism, is putting forth his protest that the world is being intellectualized by tyrants who are cultural despots. They are attempting to replace the world by ideas. They are in fact deconstructing it, emptying it of everything that does not lend itself to authority that conceives itself monolithically, nothing but consciousness.

George Orwell's explicitly old-fashioned view is that reality does start outside of us; it is in fact political. Because we are never really alone, whatever introspection tells us, power is always exerted in the name of what we have in common. Life is lived, little as some of us recognize it, as manufactured and coercive loyalties, unmistakable threats and terrible punishments, violent separations from the body politic. The sources of social control and domination are swallowed up in our anxiety, which in an age of psychology deludes itself as wholly personal and in a consumer society professing the elimination of all wants has no other goal but satisfaction. Actually, we are creatures of society, which is why the tyrant state first arises in answer to some mass deprivation. Then this tyranny that afflicts us in our name attempts to reconstitute us by forces so implacable that we internalize them. This is the aim of the Party in *Nineteen Eighty-Four*.

Nineteen Eighty-Four is in one respect an exception to the methodical social documentation that was Orwell's usual method. The most powerful details in the book relate to our identification with compulsion. The book is a prophecy, or, as Orwell said, a warning about a future terrible because it rests on a fiction and so cannot be substantiated. It would never occur to Orwell's unwearied enemy on the British left, Raymond Williams, that every pious mouthful he utters about "Socialism" is the merest abstraction couched in the in-house vocabulary of a religious sect. The book's attack on O'Brien as the Grand Inquisitor of an enforced solipsism has not been widely understood. Unlike nineteenth-century individualism, which still had some perspective on the society that was forming around it, we no longer recognize the full extent of the social controls for which we more and more live. Orwell would have enjoyed the irony. Our media culture confirms Einstein's belief that the history of an epoch is represented by its instruments. Yet nothing in the sensationalist discussion of Orwell's novel has been so mindless as television's pointing with alarm at the telescreen in *Nineteen Eighty-Four* peeking into our bedrooms. You would think that the telescreen had invented itself.

Orwell had the peculiar ability to show that social coercion affects us unconsciously. It becomes personal affliction. In *Down and Out in Paris and London* and in *The Road to Wigan Pier* he showed poverty not just as destitution but as crippling of the spirit. In *Homage To Catalonia* and in *Nineteen Eighty-Four* he demonstrated the extent to which a state at war must hold its own people hostage. What is not abstract in *Nineteen Eighty-Four* is that Winston and Julia make love under the eyes of the state, that Winston in the Ministry of Truth rewrites the past, day after day, all day long, and flogs himself to work only with the help of the Victory Gin given out at lunch with the watery stew and ersatz bread. Winston and Julia make love to the sounds of a proletarian woman in the yard singing as she does her wash. But the moment the lovers are arrested, "Something was being dragged across the stones. The woman's singing had stopped abruptly. There was a long, rolling clang, as though the washtub had been flung across the yard, and then a confusion of angry shouts which ended in a yell of pain."

Orwell's passion for the social detail—politics is how we live, how we are forced to live—was of the kind that only resistant solitary minds are capable of. "Not one of us," indeed. The social coercion that most people are no longer aware of became his fated subject because he took coercion as his personal pattern. The clue to his blunt style, with its mastery of the single sentence meant to deliver a shock, is a constant aggression on the reader. Orwell is always telling the reader how innocent everyone is about the reality of society. Orwell's specialty is his awareness of limits in all things, not least of his own talent and interest. "Truth" is his writer's ace in the hole, not imagination. Only Orwell, shot through the throat, would have made a point of saying in *Homage to Catalonia*, "I ought to say in passing that all the time I was in Spain I saw very little fighting." He clearly made up his mind very early that his ability as a writer was his ability to absorb truth in the form of pain and to give it back. In "Why I Write," a 1946 statement at the head of his *Collected Essays, Journalism and Letters*, he said that even as a boy "I knew that I had a facility with words and a power of facing unpleasant facts, and I felt that this created a sort of private world in which I could get my own back for my failure in everyday life." Writing he imagined as a "continuous" story about himself, "a sort of diary existing only in the mind." When he began writing actively, it consisted for him as a "descriptive effort almost against my will, under a kind of compulsion from [the] outside . . . always had the same meticulous descriptive quality."

Orwell remains the best commentator on his own work because he could never modify the sense of fatality behind it. Without grandiosity and without apology, he knew himself to be, vis-à-vis the unending storm of political compulsion and terror, in an exceptionally vulnerable position. "His subject matter will be determined by the age he lives in—at least this is true in tumultuous, revolutionary ages like our own—but before he ever begins to write he will have acquired an emotional attitude from which he will never completely escape." But this sense of fate made him perhaps one of the few lasting writers produced by the 1930s. Unlike Silone, Malraux, or Koestler, Orwell was never a true believer and so had nothing to repent of.

Like the stronger and more drastic Solzhenitsyn, Orwell knew why literature in the face of totalitarianism will be documentary. He knew how to face a reality entirely political. In a way, he knew nothing else. But unlike the Communist writers formed by the 1930s, Orwell also knew that good writing must be entirely consistent, that the merest touch of eclecticism or message is fatal. Literature in an age of political atrocity, as the exiles and dissidents from Eastern Europe are showing us, may take the form of fable, but the fable is designed to embarrass, to impart a sense of infliction. Orwell's sense of literature always focused on the unbearable detail. In life as in his books, he delighted in extreme gestures. In the bitter postwar winter of 1946, when fuel was scarce, Orwell actually chopped up his son's toys. But anyone who thinks that the extreme gesture in our day is found more in private life than in the state has not been reading up on the Holocaust, the Gulag, and the latest from the war between Iran and Iraq. This Orwell foretold in *Nineteen Eighty-Four*, just as brooding on Stalin as Big Brother he also imagined Khomeini. In Brazil I heard a government minister say, "We have a hundred million people in this country, most of whom we do not need." More and more leaders of the

Third World talk that way. In private many of us dream that *for* the billions of the Third World.

Orwell admitted that he was too ill when writing *Nineteen Eighty-Four* to round it all out. But of course it succeeds, it threatens, it terrorizes, because it represents a wholly oppositionist point of view that calls for the downright and repeated emphases of the great pamphleteer rather than the subtly developing action within a novel. Orwell's marked tendency to downrightedness, flatness, laying down the law, along with his powerful anticipation of fact, belongs to a radical and adversary tradition of English pamphleteering not practiced by American writers—the tradition of Swift, Tom Paine, Hazlitt, Blake, Cobbett, Chesterton, Shaw, founded on some enduring sense of injustice, on the need to break through those English class prejudices which Orwell called "a curse that confronts you like a wall of stone." Edmund Wilson used to say that the English Revolution took place in America. In Britain *literature* has been the revolution. Orwell represents this for the first half of our century as none of his countrymen do. As always, the revolution stays in just one head at a time.

Nevertheless, the great pamphleteers are the great issue raisers. Issues became Orwell's writing life, which is why even when he was near death he could never resist accepting still another book for review. His "I Write as I Please" column for *Tribune* makes up the central section of his work; the four volumes of his collected essays, letters, and journalism are more interesting to me than his novels. *Nineteen Eighty-Four*, novel or not, could have been conceived only by a pamphleteer who in his migratory life insisted on keeping his great collection of English pamphlets. His way of writing is always more or less an argument. He writes to change your mind. Socialism, which had meant justice and liberty, in its regression now forced him to choose liberty in *Nineteen Eighty-Four* as the response of "the last man in Europe" (the original title for the book) to the state's organized atrocities against a man alone.

But that is not the whole story behind *Nineteen Eighty-Four*, as Orwell bitterly insisted, just before he died, against all those attempting to turn him into a defender of the system he defined in *The Road to Wigan Pier*. "We are living in a world in which nobody is free, in which hardly anybody is secure, in which it is almost impossible to be honest and to remain alive. . . . And this is merely a preliminary stage, in a country still rich with the loot of a hundred years. Presently there may be coming God knows what horrors—horrors of which, in this sheltered island, we have not even a traditional knowledge." Rosa Luxemburg, the most trenchant critic of Lenin's despotism on the left, warned before she was murdered in 1919 that true victory lay "not at the beginning but at the end of revolution." The true radicals are those who conceive the beginning but cannot bear the end. Ignazio Silone as an exile in Switzerland used to lament: "We are the anti-Fascists, always anti! anti!" Orwell's problem was no doubt that, like so many of us, he just knew what he was against. All the more reason to take him seriously at a time when it has become unfashionable and even dangerous to be against.

Nineteen Eighty-Four: A Novel of the 1930s

by Jeffrey Meyers

The Anschluss, Guernica—all the names
At which those poets thrilled or were afraid
For me meant schools and schoolmasters and games;
And in the process someone is betrayed.
                    Donald Davie, "Remembering the Thirties"

I

Nineteen Eighty-Four is a projection of the future that is based on a concrete and naturalistic portrayal of the present and the past. Its originality is rooted in a realistic synthesis and arrangement of familiar materials rather than in prophetic and imaginary speculations.[1] The numerical title is thought to be a reversal of the last two digits of the year in which the book was completed (1948), but it was probably influenced by Yeats's poem "1919" and certainly inspired Alberto Moravia's *1934*, Anthony Burgess's *1985*, and Arthur Clarke's *2001*. If the novel had been completed a year later and the title transposed to 1994, we would have had to wait another ten years for the momentous revaluation of Orwell's work. It is notoriously difficult to predict the future accurately in a world that is rapidly transformed by technology. Who could have imagined 1949 in 1914? How precisely can we imagine 2019 in 1984?

Most of Orwell's statements about the future were not prophecies but descriptions of events that had already taken place. He looked backward in time as much as he looked forward. The portrayal of Airstrip One reflects the defeated and hopeless air of postwar London. Britain had won the war but suffered a loss of colonies and an economic decline that made the country seem worse off than its defeated enemies. The ruined, squalid, and depressing postwar city was vividly portrayed by Wyndham Lewis in *Rotting Hill* (1951). When Lewis returned to London in 1945, after six years of exile in North America, he found himself in "the capital of a dying empire—not crashing down in flames and smoke but expiring in a peculiar muffled way."[2] In 1948, the year Orwell completed his novel, Russia—recently an admired ally—had taken over all of Eastern Europe and was actively threatening the West. In that year Gandhi was assassinated, Jan Masaryk was killed (or killed himself),

Yugoslavia was expelled from the Comintern, the Berlin airlift began, Count Bernadotte was murdered in Palestine, and civil war raged in China. "It was the coup in Czechoslovakia" in 1948, writes Irving Howe, "that persuaded many people that there could be no lasting truce with the Communist world."[3]

Orwell failed to predict urban guerrillas, ecological problems, oil shortages, genetic engineering, organ transplants, computers, sophisticated spy equipment, spaceships, satellites, nuclear submarines, intercontinental missiles, and the hydrogen bomb, as well as the dissolution of empire and the postcolonial era that followed the Second World War. England and America today bear no significant resemblance to Oceania. Yet his very act of prophecy tended to induce its own fulfillment, for readers have adopted his terms and sought his portents. In the year 2000, as surely as we are now watching for Orwellian omens, masses of new believers will be standing on mountain tops waiting for the apocalypse at the end of the second millenium.

But Orwell did predict, in *Nineteen Eighty-Four*, three hostile superstates (America, Russia, and China; or NATO, the Warsaw Pact, and the nonaligned countries) engaged in permanent but limited and indecisive warfare. He said that they would use conventional weapons, that the war would be confined to peripheral territories (Central America, Africa, the Middle East, and South Asia), and that there would be no invasion of the homeland of the principal powers.[4] The Vietnam War was a classic example of America and Russia supporting foreign armies in an alien battleground. The ruthless suppression of personal freedom, the rigid indoctrination, and the widespread elimination of hostile elements during the cultural revolution in China, the Pol Pot regime in Cambodia, and the Khomeini autocracy in Iran have made *Nineteen Eighty-Four* a reality in our own time. But the horror of the Gulag Archipelago, which in 1948 had existed for nearly two decades, is far worse than anything portrayed by Orwell. Russia was like Eurasia in 1948 and it still is: a totalitarian power opposed to the West.

II

Nineteen Eighty-Four is composed of five poorly integrated elements. Orwell would have artistically refined and perfected them if he had not been desperate to finish the book before his death. He was terminally ill when he wrote the novel, had great difficulty completing it, and tried to make his task easier by repeating what he had written in his previous books. Orwell usually wrote clear drafts of his work, but more than half of the typescript of *Nineteen Eighty-Four* was crossed out and completely rewritten.[5]

The five elements are (1) a conventional Orwellian novel of poverty, frustrated love, and flight to the countryside for solitude and sex; (2) a satire on conditions in postwar England; (3) an anti-Utopian projection of an imaginary political future; (4) an almost detachable didactic argument in Goldstein's testament and the appendix on Newspeak; and (5) (the least successful and most horrible part) a portrayal of the torture and pain that are used to suppress political freedom—clearly based on his knowledge of Nazi extermination camps and his personal experience in sanatoria during 1947-48. The novel is artistically flawed because each element has a different novelistic and political purpose. How, then, do we account for the great strength of the novel, for the source of its overwhelming impact?

I have argued elsewhere that *Nineteen Eighty-Four* was influenced by Swift, Dostoyevsky, Zamyatin, and Trotsky; was a culmination of all the characteristic beliefs and ideas expressed in Orwell's works from the Depression to the Cold War; was a paradigm of the history of Europe for the previous twenty years; and expressed the political experience of an entire generation. I would now like to show that if we read *Nineteen Eighty-Four* in its cultural context— the literature of the 1930s—we can see how Orwell's various elements are connected by a unified theme. His novel is a collective text that abstracts and synthesizes all the regular and recurring elements of thirties literature. It explains the world of 1948—and by extension of 1984—by describing the conditions and ideologies that led to the Second World War.[6] In *Nineteen Eighty-Four* the 1930s were the prerevolutionary past, the final phase of capitalism that led to atomic warfare, revolution, purges, and the absolutism of Big Brother. *Nineteen Eighty-Four* is about the past as well as about the future and the present.

The past is one of the dominant themes of the novel. The Party confidently believes: "Who controls the past controls the future: who controls the present controls the past." The Party can not only change the past but can also destroy it and authoritatively state: "it never happened."[7] By creating a new as well as destroying the old past, the Party can also arrange to predict events that have already taken place. Winston spends a great deal of time conversing with the proles, trying to recall and reestablish the personal and historical past that has been officially abolished, for he believes that the past may still exist in human memory. When Winston plots with O'Brien, they drink "To the past." O'Brien gravely agrees that the past is more important than the future because under a system of organized lying only a remembrance of the past can prevent the disappearance of objective truth.

Orwell's ideas about the capacity of language to express complex thoughts and feelings, to describe the dimensions of experience with accuracy and honesty, are central to *Nineteen Eighty-Four*. These ideas originate in Winston's desire to rediscover his own past—in his dreams and his diary—and are contrasted to Ampleforth's enthusiastic creation of Newspeak. In pursuing these thoughts about language, Orwell joined the literary debate about modern prose.

The Newspeak tendency to reduce the language, to limit the meaning, and to reject abstract words was originally a positive aspect of modern prose that developed just after the Great War. Hemingway, who began his career as a journalist, was fascinated by the language of telegraphic cables that resembles the messages sent to Winston's desk at the Ministry of Truth: "speech malreported africa rectify." Hemingway told his colleague Lincoln Steffens: "Stef, look at this cable: no fat, no adjectives, no adverbs—nothing but blood and bones and muscle. It's great. It's a new language."[8] Influenced by Ezra Pound, Hemingway came to believe: "Prose is architecture, not interior decoration, and the Baroque is over."[9]

Like Robert Graves, John Dos Passos, Erich Remarque, and other writers who had served in the Great War, Hemingway learned to distrust patriotic rhetoric. In *A Farewell to Arms* he wrote: "I was always embarrassed by the words sacred, glorious, and sacrifice and the expression in vain. . . . Abstract words such as glory, honor, courage, or hallow were obscene beside the concrete names of villages, the numbers of roads, the names of rivers, the numbers of regiments and the dates."[10] The abstractions were lies. Only the concrete places where men had fought and died had any dignity and meaning. The bitter disillusionment of the Great War is connected to the betrayal of principles in *Nineteen Eighty-Four* by Winston's prophecy of doom: "We are the dead," which is repeated by Julia and reaffirmed by the telescreen when they are arrested. For Winston's grim phrase is an ironic echo of an accusatory line, spoken by a corpse, from John Macrae's popular poem of the First World War, "In Flanders Fields":

We are the Dead. Short days ago
We lived, felt dawn, saw sunset glow,
  Loved and were loved, and now we lie
    In Flanders fields.[11]

In the thirties, this need to reject meaningless abstractions was combined with the desire to find a basic vocabulary and create a proletarian literature. Though Hemingway's short words, limited vocabulary, and declarative sentences, his bare, clear, and forceful style, had a salutary effect on modern prose, he was criticized by Wyndham Lewis in "The Dumb Ox" for choking off the possibilities of thought: "Hemingway invariably invokes a dull-witted, bovine, monosyllabic simpleton . . . a super-innocent, queerly-sensitive, village-idiot of a few words and fewer ideas."[12] *Nineteen Eighty-Four* demonstrates how the modern tendency to reduce language to its essential meaning can, when carried to the extremes of Newspeak, make the expression of unorthodox opinions almost impossible.

Orwell's essay "Politics and the English Language" demonstrates the connection between inaccurate expression and dishonest thought. It debunks political pomposity, criticizes fuzzy thinking, and shows the corruption that comes from the use of clichés, hackneyed diction, and dead language. *Nineteen Eighty-Four*, however, criticizes the opposite tendency to oversimplify language so that it limits the range of human expression. While expounding the principles of Newspeak and creating the brilliant neologisms that have taken a permanent place in our speech (*Big Brother*, *Thought Police*, *doublethink*, *facecrime*, *vaporized*, *unperson*), Orwell also predicted the radical deterioration of language and the perversion of meaning. In our time, the influence of technology, bureaucracy, television, and journalism has debased the language. Dangerous euphemisms have diminished the reality of all unpleasant concepts: *prison, torture, war, disease, old age,* and *death.* Vague but condemnatory words—*Communist, fascist, racist, sexist*—have been indiscriminately attached to anything that anyone dislikes. Orwell would have deplored the primacy of visual over verbal media in our culture—television and video over books and magazines—and the corruption of language by computer jargon. All these tendencies have produced words that seem to be written on a typewriter by a typewriter.

III

Many of the characteristic literary themes of the thirties appear in *Nineteen Eighty-Four*: schools, cinema, advertising and propaganda, public issues, self-deception, Marx and Freud, violence and war. And aspects of Orwell's reportage—his anatomy of Burma, France, and England in the 1930s in "A Hanging," "How the Poor Die," and *The Road to Wigan Pier*—are incorporated in *Nineteen Eighty-Four* to provide the documentary basis of the future world.

The writers of the 1930s had intense feelings about the conventions and codes of schools and schoolboys, which were often based on their personal experiences as both teachers and pupils. The headmaster became the embodiment of social and political power, and the austerity and sadism of the school were contrasted to the civility and kindness of the home. Auden expressed this theme when he wrote: "The best reason I have for opposing Fascism is that at school I lived in a Fascist state."[13] Anthony West, who described his own horrible schooldays in the autobiographical novel *Heritage*, was the first to notice that "most of these [terrors], in *Nineteen Eighty-Four*, are of an infantile character, and they clearly derive from the experience described in *Such, Such Were the Joys*. . . . What he did in *Nineteen Eighty-Four* was to send everybody in England to an enormous Crossgates to be as miserable as he had been."[14]

Nineteen Eighty-Four explores the complex mixture of nostalgia, fear, and self-hatred that Orwell felt when writing about his school days. By drawing on these intense early experiences, he convincingly portrays the psychological effects of totalitarian oppression: isolation, enforced group activities, physical discomfort, desire to suck up to those in power, lack of identity, and feelings of guilt. The physical exercises, sexual propaganda, songs, processions, banners, and drills all derive from school. Parsons, who resembles a large boy, is an athletic Hearty. Winston dislikes Julia at first "because of the atmosphere of hockey-fields and cold baths and community hikes and general cleanmindedness which she managed to carry about with her." Even Winston's compulsive repetition of DOWN WITH BIG BROTHER in his diary recalls the lines written out as punishment at school.

Nineteen Eighty-Four reflects the 1930s ritual of cinema-going and the cult of film stars; the interest in advertising and the use of propaganda. In *Keep the Aspidistra Flying*, Gordon Comstock hates the movies and seldom goes there. But a recurring image in *Nineteen Eighty-Four* is the bombing of Jewish refugees in the Mediterranean which Winston sees at the cinema on April 3, 1984. Several hundred victims are killed when a rocket bomb falls on a crowded film theater in Stepney, East London. The obligatory Two Minutes Hate, with Goldstein as the star performer, is projected on a gigantic telescreen before a hysterical anti-Semitic audience.[15]

Winston dimly recalls an advertisement for wine in which "a vast bottle composed of electric lights seemed to move up and down and pour its contents into a glass." Virtually all the Outer Party members are swallowers of slogans: "War is Peace / Freedom is Slavery / Ignorance is Strength." (Should not it logically be "Ignorance is Wisdom"?) As in a modern political campaign, the head of Big Brother (whose image is an amalgam of Stalin and Kitchener) appears "on coins, on stamps, on the covers of books, on banners, on posters, and on the wrapping of a cigarette packet—everywhere."

The writers of the thirties dealt with public themes. It was a decade of economic depression throughout the world; massive unemployment and poverty; the misery of democracies and the rise of fascism; wars in Manchuria, Ethiopia, and Spain; the Nazi seizure of territory in Austria, Czechoslovakia, and Poland. Russia experienced the forced collectivization of the Kulaks (1929-33), the Ukraine famine (1933), the exile and the murder of Trotsky (1940), and the Great Purge Trials (1936-38). Writers fared badly under totalitarianism; Mayakovsky, Babel, and Mandelshtam were killed during Stalin's regime. The decade of hatred between the Nazis and the Communists culminated in profound disillusionment with the Hitler-Stalin non-aggression pact (August 1939), which was repudiated by Germany's invasion of Russia (June 1941). This abrupt alteration of political alliances was portrayed in *Nineteen Eighty-Four* when "it became known, with extreme suddenness and everywhere at once, that Eastasia and not Eurasia was the enemy. . . . The Hate continued exactly as before, except that the target had been changed."

As in 1930s literature, intellectuals in *Nineteen Eighty-Four* lie to support their cause and protect their own position, agree to accept and practice immoral acts. Orwell once condemned Auden for his phrase "the necessary murder." In *Nineteen Eighty-Four* O'Brien asks Winston: "If, for example, it would somehow serve our interests to throw sulphuric acid in a child's face—are you prepared to do that?" and he unhesitatingly answers: "Yes." In both the 1930s and in *Nineteen Eighty-Four* the ruling class betrays the principles of the revolution, the deceivers are themselves deceived.

The committed writers of the 1930s developed a new moral awareness and literary strategy to deal with the dreadful conditions of the time. They became socially and politically conscious, and abandoned private art for public communication. They adopted a new tone and rhetoric in which to express their new convictions and often embraced left-wing or Communist ideology. The two main intellectual influences of the thirties, Marx and Freud, are faithfully reflected in *Nineteen Eighty-Four*. The Marxist dialectic, expressed in Trotsky's style, appears in the forbidden tract, *The Theory and Practice of Oligarchical Collectivism*. Winston embraces the Marxist belief: "If there was hope, it must lie in the proles." His hope is not based on their real or theoretical virtue, but on the fact that they comprise eighty-five percent of the population and are the only force that seems strong enough to overthrow the Party. But the proles lack a Marxist political awareness and a desire to revolt against oppression.

Orwell suggests a Freudian interpretation of Winston's dreams to depict his inner life. They concern Winston's guilt about the sacrificial death of his mother, which foreshadows his betrayal of Julia. Winston realizes that the political hysteria stirred up by the Two Minutes Hate is an emotional outlet for "sex gone sour." And the last line of the children's poem, which he has been vainly trying to remember, is supplied by the voice on the telescreen when he and Julia are arrested in their secret bedroom. The line suggests the threat of castration after sexual pleasure: "Here comes a candle to light you to bed, here comes a chopper to chop off your head!"

In the thirties violence was used to achieve political ends. The strong dictator replaced God as the omnipotent figure and ruled with absolute and intimidating power. There were constant threats of bombing civilians and of global war. Gordon Comstock eagerly awaits this destruction in *Keep the Aspidistra Flying*; George Bowling dreads it in *Coming Up for Air*. In *Nineteen Eighty-Four* the rocket bombs are fired on the people by their own government in order to arouse continuous hatred of the enemy. The confrontation of Communism and fascism in Spain was, for most intellectuals, their first real experience in politics and warfare. Auden and Spender attended propaganda conferences in Spain; Hemingway and Koestler went as journalists; Francis Cornford and Julian Bell were killed. But of all the major writers involved in the war, only Orwell fought as a common soldier, was seriously wounded, and survived to record his experiences. He came from the generation which had failed The Test by being too young to participate in the Great War, but he brilliantly passed The Test in Spain. Orwell (and his wife) knew from personal experience what it felt like to be hunted by the secret police. His honesty and integrity shine through *Nineteen Eighty-Four* as they did in the literary personae of the more openly autobiographical works of the thirties. All his books project what Malcolm Muggeridge has called "his proletarian fancy dress, punctilious rolling of his cigarettes, his rusty laugh and woebegone expression and kindly disposition."[16]

IV

Even more effective than evoking the past world of the thirties to explain the evolution of 1948 and 1984 is Orwell's ironic and cruel reversal of the dominant political themes of the period: homosexuality, frontiers, spies, technology, Mass Observation, change of consciousness, collective action, justification of Communism and intellectual polarities. Winston affirms Orwell's own commendable heresies of the 1930s: his refusal to adopt the orthodoxy of the left about the socialist intelligentsia in England (criticized in *The Road to Wigan Pier*) and about the Communist Party in Spain (condemned in *Homage to Catalonia*). *Nineteen Eighty-Four* contains two opposing strains: Orwell's truthful revelations about the horrors of both fascism and Communism, and his despair about the destruction of the hopes and ideals of the thirties.

The homosexual theme, founded on adolescent love affairs in school, portrayed as a protest against the oppressive educational system and idealized in poems like Auden's "Lay your sleeping head," becomes perversely twisted in *Nineteen Eighty-Four*. Winston's intense attachment to O'Brien takes on homosexual overtones and verges on sexcrime. (When tortured, Winston freely but falsely admits he is a sexual pervert.) When he first comes to his hero's flat, "A wave of admiration, almost of worship, flowed out from Winston towards O'Brien." When O'Brien tortures him to the point of lunacy and death, "It made no difference. In some sense that went deeper than friendship, they were intimates." And just before he faces his final degradation in Room 101, "The peculiar reverence for O'Brien, which nothing seemed able to destroy, flooded Winston's heart again." Like the young favorite of the Head Boy at school, Winston vacillates between craven submission and a lust for vicarious power.

O'Brien's Irish name may have been inspired by the surname of Orwell's first wife, Eileen O'Shaughnessy, by her brother Dr. Eric Lawrence O'Shaughnessy (who had the same Christian name as Orwell) and by Eric's wife, Dr. Gwen O'Shaughnessy. The name may have expressed Orwell's fears about the power, domination, and sexual demands of women, which the passive Winston is scarcely able to deal with. Eileen, as closely attached to her brother as to her husband, was deeply grieved by Eric's death at Dunkirk in 1941. Both Eric and Gwen O'Shaughnessy treated Orwell for tuberculosis in the 1930s. Orwell may have transferred his antagonism from the doctors—who seemed to be torturing him while trying to cure him during the unsuccessful treatment with streptomycin in 1948—to the authoritarian figure of O'Brien. While curing Winston of thoughtcrime, O'Brien destroys his body exactly as the doctors had done.

The map, the frontier, and the geographical context were recurrent metaphors in the poetry of Auden and his followers. The marked increase of this imagery coincided with the obsolescence of the frontier, which was easily overrun by tanks, planes, and modern armies. (Goldstein declares: "The main frontiers must never be crossed by anything except bombs.") Orwell sets his novel in a global context by describing two vast land masses that are alternately opposed to and aligned with Oceania. A Flying Fortress lies between Iceland and the Faroes in the north; victories are announced on the Malabar front in the south; and the permanent land wars take place in the rough quadrilateral covered by Tangier, Brazzaville, Darwin, and Hong Kong. Julia gives Winston precise directions to their secret meeting place "as though she had a map inside her head." And Orwell is concerned, more profoundly than the thirties writers, with the inner psychic frontier at which man can be broken and made to betray.

In the literature of the 1930s spies secretly cross the frontier and operate independently against the alien population. In *Nineteen Eighty-Four* Goldstein is said to control spies and saboteurs; but the real Spies (the name of a youth group) work in the home against their own parents. Parsons, the most enthusiastic Party hack, is proud of the fact that his daughter has betrayed him for uttering "Down with Big Brother" in his sleep (another example of the Freudian unconscious at work). All the principal characters in the novel are either arrested (Winston, Julia, Parsons, Syme, Ampleforth) or work for the Thought Police (O'Brien, Charrington, Parsons's daughter).

The thirties writers, following the Italian futurists, were fascinated by modernism, airplanes, and technological advance. Auden liked industrial landscapes and advocated "New styles of architecture, a change of heart." Orwell, who "loved the past, hated the present and dreaded the future,"[17] opposed modern change and longed for the familiar cosiness of the decent past. In *Nineteen Eighty-Four* a dehumanized London is called Airstrip One and hovering helicopters snoop into people's windows. Technology either breaks down and causes chaos or operates efficiently and leads to repression.

The characteristic mode of social inquiry in the 1930s was Tom Harrisson's Mass Observation, which "tried to understand social behavior by accumulating disparate [factual] observations about what given groups of people were doing."[18] This is also ironically reversed in *Nineteen Eighty-Four* where Mass Observation is a mode of surveillance carried on by the Thought Police to identify and vaporize potential opponents of the regime.

The writers of the 1930s advocated a change of heart and new awareness that would lead to revolutionary commitment. In *Nineteen Eighty-Four* there is also an alteration of consciousness and a commitment to the revolution—but of an entirely different kind. In the last part of the novel, O'Brien tortures Winston—using a process that resembles Electro-Convulsive Therapy—in order to humiliate him and destroy his powers of reasoning. He makes Winston believe that $2 + 2 = 5$, forces him to betray Julia, crushes him until he loves Big Brother.

The idea of collective action was a major preoccupation of the thirties. Writers were concerned with relating the public and private dimensions of their lives, with creating a Popular Front, with establishing a secure defense against fascism by immersing themselves in the collective security of the Soviet Union. In the 1930s there "was an attempt to deny utterly the validity of individual knowledge and observation."[19] Unlike most writers of the 1930s, Orwell (who had served as part of a unit in the Burma Police) rejected the idea of collective action and almost always stood alone. The only group he ever joined—the Anarchists in Spain—were an underdog minority, destined for destruction. Like all left writers of the thirties, Orwell hoped for a new social order; but he did not believe that Communism would help mankind progress toward that goal. In *Nineteen Eighty-Four* the Party embodies the collective mind and all members are forced to participate in communal activities. Winston, locked in loneliness, becomes a lunatic, a minority of one, the only man still capable of independent thought. He is "The Last Man in Europe" (the original title of the book) precisely because he adheres to the importance of the individual mind. Orwell shows that totalitarianism paradoxically intensifies solitude by forcing all the isolated beings into one overpowering system.

Thirties writers idealized and justified the Soviet Union—even after the transcripts of the Purge Trials had been published and the pact with Hitler signed. They argued that any criticism of Russia was objectively pro-fascist. This belief was carried to a typically ludicrous extreme in a line of Day Lewis's "The Road These Times Must Take": "Yes, why do we all, seeing a communist, feel small?" Winston feels small when he sees O'Brien, not only because he admires and loves him, but because he craves O'Brien's power ("The object of power is power") and is reduced by his torture to a rotten, suppurating cadaver who resembles "a man of sixty, suffering from some malignant disease." In *Nineteen Eighty-Four* Winston's physical disease symbolizes his intellectual "illness": his heretical hatred of the prevailing ideology.

Finally, the political conditions of the 1930s led to an intellectual polarity between catastrophe and rebirth, a contrast between economic and industrial collapse and revolutionary hope for the future, a belief in the destruction of the old social order for the sake of a new Communist world. *Nineteen Eighty-Four* combines and transforms these polarities. The revolution is followed by betrayal and repression, catastrophe leads only to catastrophe, the new order is far worse than the old. In Orwell's novel, the "endless catalogue of atrocities, massacres, deportations, lootings, rapings, torture of prisoners, bombing of civilians, lying propaganda, unjust aggressions, broken treaties" are attributed to Eurasia (or Eastasia), but they actually take place in Oceania.

After the Second World War, the destruction of much of England, the reaffirmation of the class system, and his own long illness, Orwell realized that the totalitarian states he had written about in his essay on James Burnham had come into permanent existence. The ideas of the 1930s had led to the chaos of postwar Europe and his hopes had been destroyed. Orwell's disillusionment and disease help to account for the political ideas and the artistic flaws of the novel. *Nineteen Eighty-Four* is at once a warning about the future, a satire on the present, and an ironic parody of the literary and political themes of the thirties. The past, as a theoretical concept and a historical reality, is crucial to the meaning of the novel. "The best books, [Winston] perceived, are those that tell you what you know already."

Notes

1. See Jeffrey Meyers, "The Genesis of *1984*," *A Reader's Guide to George Orwell* (London: Thames & Hudson, 1975), 144-54. See also Jeffrey Meyers, *George Orwell: The Critical Heritage* (London: Routledge & Kegan Paul, 1975), and Jeffrey and Valerie Meyers, *George Orwell: An Annotated Bibliography of Criticism* (New York: Garland, 1977).
2. Letter from Wyndham Lewis to Geoffrey Stone, January 15, 1948, quoted in Jeffrey Meyers, *The Enemy: A Biography of Wyndham Lewis* (London: Routledge & Kegan Paul, 1980), 286.
3. Irving Howe, *Celebrations and Attacks* (London: Deutsch, 1979), 208-9.
4. Since 1948, wars have been fought in Korea, Vietnam, Cambodia, Laos, Malaya, Indonesia, Israel, Egypt, Jordan, Syria, Lebanon, Cyprus, Yemen, Iran, Iraq, the Congo, Kenya, Sudan, Nigeria, Ethiopia, Somalia, Angola, Mozambique, Rhodesia, Chad, Chile, Nicaragua, El Salvador, and the Falkland Islands.
5. I have examined a microfilm copy of the typescript of *Nineteen Eighty-Four* in the Orwell Archive at University College, London University. The original is in a private collection in America and will be published in a facsimile edition by Harcourt, Brace in 1984.
6. The standard works on this period are Samuel Hynes, *The Auden Generation* (London: Bodley Head, 1976) and Bernard Bergonzi, *Reading the Thirties* (London: Macmillan, 1978).
7. George Orwell, *Nineteen Eighty-Four* (London: Penguin, 1972), 31.
8. Letter from George Seldes to Jeffrey Meyers, April 2, 1983.
9. Ernest Hemingway, *Death in the Afternoon* (New York: Scribner's, 1932), 191.
10. Ernest Hemingway, *A Farewell to Arms* (New York: Scribner's, 1969), 184-85.
11. John Macrae, "In Flanders Fields," *The Oxford Book of Canadian Verse* (Toronto: Oxford University Press, 1960), 110.
12. Wyndham Lewis, "The Dumb Ox," *Life and Letters* (April 1934), reprinted in Jeffrey Meyers, *Hemingway: The Critical Heritage* (London: Routledge & Kegan Paul, 1982), 196-97.
13. W. H. Auden in *The Old School*, ed. Graham Greene (London: Jonathan Cape, 1934), 14.
14. Anthony West, "George Orwell," *Principles and Persuasions* (London: Eyre & Spottiswoode, 1958), 156, 158.
15. See Jeffrey Meyers, "Orwell as Film Critic," *Sight and Sound* 48 (Autumn 1979), 255-56.
16. Malcolm Muggeridge, "Langham Diary," *Listener*, October 6, 1983, p. 18.
17. Malcolm Muggeridge, quoted in Meyers, *Reader's Guide to George Orwell*, p. 144.
18. Bergonzi, *Reading the Thirties*, 52.
19. Julian Symons, *The Thirties: A Dream Revolved* (London: Faber and Faber, 1960), 142.

Discussion

Discussion was opened by a question from the floor whether there was a rejection in England, similar to that in the United States, of 1920s writers by 1930s writers. Mr. KAZIN said there was not, despite the "enormous strength of Communist intellectuals and writers in the 1930s in England." Citing the English caste system as a reason, he said that "people like Waugh, Chesterton, and a great many actively anti-left" intellectuals were able to remain "safe, secure, and contemptuous in their own literary places." Mr. DONOGHUE finds Orwell's reception by the English left of "very great significance" and referred to an argument that has been going on for the past several years among English left-wing writers, who are exasperated with Orwell and "with what they regard as the sinister use to which *Nineteen Eighty-Four* was put, notably in America, by sponsors of the right who turned the book into a parable saying, 'Didn't we tell you so?' " Mr. DONOGHUE thinks that the English left greatly resents Orwell's "privileged access to the truth": "he knew what truth was, what a historical fact was, what historical meaning was," and that Orwell "nefariously laid claim to . . . moral significance but did not earn the right to possess it." Mr. KAZIN here drew another England/ U.S. distinction: whereas in America, a "tremendous army of ex-leftists" still consider themselves "somehow socialists in some ideal sense," on the other hand in England John Strachey, author of one of the most influential books of the 1930s, *The Coming Struggle for Power*, changed into "a very conventional, active anti-Russian and a very useful war minister." In England, Mr. Strachey was considered "perfectly safe," because he belonged to the "right class," whereas in the United States "nobody would think of employing Norman Podhoretz, Lionel Trilling, or James Burnham in positions of governmental power." Mr. CRICK from the floor sought but failed to gain Mr. DONOGHUE's agreement that "rejection of Orwell by the English left is on the wane." Mr. CRICK cited his own forty or fifty invitations from Labour Party groups in the past year to speak on Orwell, including one from the "most pro-Marxist group in the country, the Labour Party for Sheffield City Council, to give their Marx Memorial Lecture." Mr. DONOGHUE observed that "Kinnockian Labour would not be regarded as of the left," nor be "endorsed . . . by people like Terry Eagleton" and other writers of the *New Left Review*, who "would certainly not regard the present Labour Party as in any way representing his hopes or aspirations." Indeed, to the contrary, Mr. DONOGHUE said, Mr. CRICK's many Labour Party invitations to speak on Orwell only point to the "gross discontinuity between the sentiments which were entrusted to the left in the thirties and forties and what has happened to those sentiments now: those sentiments have moved to the center. . . . The Labour Party represents itself, I think, unashamedly indeed, as a party of the center." Mr. CRICK: "Not so! I write speeches for Mr. Kinnock on occasion, and he represents himself as in the tradition of Aneurin Bevan."

Here Mr. KAZIN asked to bring the discussion back to why Orwell was "hated so much." Mr. KAZIN distinguished the "good English radical, the Labour radical" ("the Labour Party intellectuals always *think* they have a program") from George Orwell, whom Mr. KAZIN calls a "moral radical, in a tradition which is very Protestant, very English," reminiscent to Mr. KAZIN of "William Blake because it was so abstract . . . so moral, and really evangelical." Orwell, according to Mr. KAZIN, cared not about "the bread-and-butter issue specifically" but about "the moral end of socialism" as "defined so beautifully" by Marx and by Nicola Chiaromonte: " 'The idea is to transform human relationships.' They did not mean the welfare state; [they] meant a new way of living with other people, a new sense of life." Mr. KAZIN said he was amused to hear C. P. Snow, "who hated Orwell bitterly," defending "the infamous Stalinist novelist Sholokhov" when Snow had just come back from Russia and denouncing George Orwell. "I thought it was a perfect example of the way in which the good English radical, the Labour radical, had it both ways, you see."

There was a question whether the French have changed at all since the late forties, "with Sartre and now the people . . . associated with Mitterand," specifically whether *Nineteen Eighty-Four* is being discussed in France. Mr. STANSKY mentioned that a "huge conference" on Orwell in Strasbourg, France, was recently convened by the Council of Europe. Another question from the floor inquiring why *Nineteen Eighty-Four* is "being so widely revived this year" elicited from Mr. KAZIN: "Because [Orwell] left an enduring image of our time, which only a great writer ever does"; (from EDWARD WEISMILLER from the floor): "whether or not it is a flawed novel, or structurally imperfect, or a political fable, maybe it couldn't possibly be better than it is. The fact is, we're here. We are all indelibly moved by, and indelibly colored by this book." Mr. MEYERS, pointing out that the book could have been better, specified among "many things" that Orwell did not do to "achieve something like artistic perfection": "a lot of melodramatic and horror stuff could be toned down; the characters of Winston and Julia could have been deepened and made more complicated, just to name two things"; from Mr. STANSKY: "It's a nice irony that Orwell wanted to avoid . . . the 'clichéd reaction,' " but on the other hand it is "an immediate clichéd reaction, almost a jargon reaction: the year is 1984, therefore we have all these conferences;" from Mr. MEYERS: "1984 evokes Orwell; he cornered the year well in advance, and then we waited . . . [but] the answer is in the kind of man he was as much as what he wrote. . . . Looking into writers' lives usually diminishes them in some way . . . and very few writers can stand up to the kind of scrutiny that we give them . . . but when we look very closely at Orwell, we like him more. We don't find many flaws, and even the flaws are rather charming and eccentric and cranky, and there's a consistency and harmony in the way he embodies the values in his life that he seems to be admiring in his works. . . . [This is why] I'm interested in him, let's put it that way, and I would imagine that's true for other people, too." Mr. KAZIN sees the current interest, excitement, distress, and proliferating conferences concerning Orwell and his work as directly related to the "total political anxiety of our time . . . the tremendous unconscious political anxiety, not least in this country . . . because of what we're going through right now." Mr. CRICK averred that Orwell's "genius lies in his essays," that "*Nineteen Eighty-Four* is not [his] best work," and disagreed with Mr. MEYERS's argument that Orwell was a "nice person. . . . I didn't feel he was, but I felt he was a great writer. . . . Some of his English pals—his Bloomsbury pals and his Chelsea pals, who were very uncomfortable with this airy kind of writing, began to build up the image [of Orwell] as the simple, innocent man, the Douanier Rousseau of English letters. I think that is rubbish." Mr. KAZIN added that Orwell was very aggressive—"imagine calling a fellow writer a 'gutless Kipling,' imagine referring to the 'pansy left' "—but holds that we're interested in Orwell because "the thirties have become, for obvious reasons, one of the most derogated periods in history, and [the thirties] deserve to be rehabilitated because of the dream on the left, which he never gave up. . . . That's why we remember him as we remember Silone and very few others. If you compare what Orwell wrote on the Spanish Civil War with what was being published in *New Statesman* in this period . . . you recognize that he was of the thirties but definitely not part of the gang that controlled things at that time." Mr. MEYERS said Winston's fate is "living proof that the system can triumph over the individual, and that he can be sent back to society, not as a renegade but as somebody who is now working for the cause; so he's an example of the system working well and also at the same time a warning."

In reply to a question from the floor whether *Nineteen Eighty-Four* is a novel or a fable, and whether it is closer to the fabulous when compared with *Brave New World*, Mr. DONOGHUE said that *Nineteen Eighty-Four* is closer to fable than novel and also closer to the fabulous when compared with *Brave New World*, despite our contemporary lack of critical flair for reading fable. Because our sense of literature, rightly or wrongly, is very predominantly based on the novel ("its notion of realism and the primacy of the political"), we "simply don't know how to read *Tale of a Tub*, and I'm not sure we're much more agile in knowing how to read *Gulliver's Travels*." A complication "adding to the intriguing force of Orwell . . . is that he occupies a very strange position. On the one hand he was what the Germans would call 'a punctual writer' . . . addressing himself to the [journalistic and pamphleteering] immediacies . . . the particular events of the moment, and yet at the same time he was an artist maintaining, not perhaps impeccably, but maintaining to a very high degree that stance of distance without which the composition of a fable is impossible." There are other writers in whom one might also observe this mixture of fabulist and punctualist (Silone; ALFRED KAZIN has mentioned Chiaromonte), but "the fact that we have to dredge around to make these comparisons shows how strange, improbable, and infrequent such a writer is. . . . And I think this partly gives us some reason for the strange authoritativeness that we concede to Orwell. I agree with ALFRED KAZIN that it is indeed because of the political resonance *Nineteen Eighty-Four* has, but I think that that also has to do with that strange intermediate status or location which Orwell achieved for himself." Ms. CALDER added that, rather than trying to fit him into one novelistic category or another, we should see him as belonging to the very ancient tradition of the storyteller responding to events and absorbing them into a continuous narrative, whether that narrative is fiction or nonfiction; in effect, a historian of the contemporary scene. From the floor came the query, under the test that thirty-six years separate 1948 and 1984, whether we could write such a book in 1984 looking forward to 2020 and in that book have as much power and authority as *Nineteen Eighty-Four*. To Mr. KAZIN the decisive word is *authority*, and he went on to compare Orwell's investment of his own isolation and personal suffering with the same kind of "moral authority" as that of Nicola Chiaromonte and Ignazio Silone. Mr. KAZIN continued: "[Orwell] raised the question, which only the young Karl Marx ever raised before him, namely, is there a chance that mankind will ever get away from distraction of the economic struggle for existence, get back to the real problem, which Goethe defined perfectly as a sense of awe which man feels before the universe itself. . . . [Orwell] said . . . that we have to achieve socialism, whatever that may be, in order to get away from the economic struggle and get back 'to the sense of absolute right and wrong.' . . . Anyone who knows American literature today knows that for many years now, religion, a sense of right and wrong, has not preoccupied our writers. . . . But a century ago, Emerson and Thoreau and Melville were concerned with nothing else. And Orwell . . . would have felt, as Camus did, that something was missing from our literature because of that. And why? Because we're so completely dominated by the struggle for existence, which socialism was supposed to end. Well, in *Nineteen Eighty-Four*, the struggle for existence is over. There are no problems any more, except how to stay alive, and that's what Orwell was getting at."

In reply to a question from the floor whether Upton Sinclair might be a parallel American writer, Mr. KAZIN dismissed Sinclair as "a parody of the novelist *engagé*," and hoped the conference would address the subject of why "the English have great pamphleteers and we don't. . . . In America we had only one figure like [Chesterton and Shaw], William James . . . who was a great writer moving in the realm of polemic and moral issues all the time. Our writers of the thirties were on the whole a pretty sad lot." Mr. MEYERS called D. H. Lawrence the "closest to Orwell in touching issues that are important today. Not the same issues that Orwell did, but relations between the sexes, love, freedom, social class . . . and he's alive today in the way Orwell is. But, again, I can't think of an American quite like Orwell." Mr. KAZIN considers Mark Twain "perhaps . . . [whose] most extraordinary pamphlets were not published during his lifetime. He was afraid to publish them." Mr. CRICK commented that Orwell once wanted to write a popular life of Mark Twain.

Mr. KAZIN, asked from the floor to elaborate on Orwell's attitude toward the United States, replied that upon seeing in *Vogue* magazine a picture of a tailor on his knees fixing the hem of a lady's dress, Orwell wrote "bitterly and savagely and contemptuously that this was the attitude of American men to the American woman, which he felt was deplorable."

From the floor, someone observed that the writers "who could have been the Orwells in the United States" were mainly concerned with literary criticism, so that perhaps the books from the 1930s and early 1940s that are going to last are works of literary criticism. Of two other writers put forward from the floor as comparable to Orwell, Mr. KAZIN said of Edmund Wilson: "He certainly is, but Wilson lost all interest and belief in the regeneration of humanity [and] was an almost embarrassingly aggressive atheist [whose] opinions about Orwell were significantly indecisive for that very reason"; and of Nathanael West: "Orwell was not mordant the way Nathanael West was, about Hollywood, about everything else." Mr. KAZIN closed by commenting that "socialism in America has not, for a number of years, had any real meaning whatsoever; whereas in England, it's still a great, great moral force and movement."

Nineteen Eighty-Four:
Its Meaning Today

The Reception of *Nineteen Eighty-Four*

by Bernard Crick

Orwellian conveys gloom and pessimism, at the best dark warnings; but *Orwell-like* conveys simplicity, straightforwardness and both a love of nature and naturalness. For a man famous for his plain style who prided himself on simplicity of expression, varying interpretations of *Nineteen Eighty-Four* both now and at the time of publication are astonishing. It has been read as a deterministic prophecy, as a conditional projection of what might happen, as a humanistic satire of contemporary events, as religious allegory, as nihilistic misanthropy, as total rejection of socialism, and as a libertarian-socialist, almost anarchist, protest against totalitarian tendencies both in his own and other societies. Some read it literally, some as a satire, some ideological body-snatchers come from the right and some from the left.

Some of these ambiguities have arisen because almost from the beginning, people type-cast Orwell as a simple, straightforward man who happened to write simple, straightforward books. It should be quite obvious that *Nineteen Eighty-Four* as a text is anything but straightforward; it is a highly complex text. So it is then thought that Orwell was over-reaching himself, or was in a kind of inspired depression. I simply assume, however, that Orwell was a highly self-conscious literary artist who deliberately set out to achieve very much the effects he did achieve.

In the end, Orwell fully succeeded in his deepest ambition: to be a popular novelist. Indeed, he is almost all that is left of our common culture as regards the printed word rather than the broadcast media: he is still read for pleasure and instruction by an audience almost as wide and diverse as once read Dickens, Mark Twain, and H.G. Wells, writers on whom he modelled himself. The plain style he developed was to reach the common man, not to reach other intellectuals. There is an irony in his career, in that each of his prewar novels, written for the common man, reached very few people indeed—none selling more than three to four thousand copies. But *Nineteen Eighty-Four*, like *Animal Farm*, reached a huge audience, an audience incidentally the vast majority of whom did not know his earlier works, nor where he stood politically. The satirist must know his audience; Orwell's very success moved him onto dangerous ground. However, there are many indications that in *Nineteen Eighty-Four* he was trying to write a novel that would appeal both to the old common reader, say the public library reading classes, not the intellectuals, but also to literary intellectuals. He was trying to write a modern, futurist novel in the style of traditional naturalism. *Nineteen Eighty-Four* is the most ambitious and complex work that Orwell attempted, not entirely successfully.

Take simply the famous opening paragraph: "It was a bright cold day in April, and the clocks were striking thirteen. Winston Smith, his chin nuzzled into his breast in an effort to escape the vile wind, slipped quickly through the glass doors of the Victory Mansions, though not quickly enough to prevent a swirl of gritty dust from entering along with him." The common reader, who would be appalled and disoriented, or rather appalled because he was disoriented, by the opening paragraph of James Joyce's *Ulysses*, should feel thoroughly at home, more or less. He is told the time of year, the temperature, given the name of the hero and precise physical location. Nonetheless, there is something strange, not merely that it is a cold day in April, but that the clocks are striking thirteen. Great Britain was fully conversant with the "continental" twenty-four hour clock during the war and afterwards, but it was only used for official purposes; it never became colloquial, nor was it on the faces of clocks until the recent digital era. When clocks strike thirteen, we are either in the future or in a fairy tale. "Winston Smith" couples the most common name in the English language with the most famous. The "vile wind" and "gritty dust" counteract the cheerful futurist image of "glass doors" and make one wonder if there were "Victory Mansions," what kind of pyrrhic victory it was. We are entering into a futurist regime, yet it is not one of gleaming white concrete, steel, glass, and synthetics, such as Wells had loved to picture: it is a crumbling dust-strewn decay (much like, of course, immediate postwar London). Even in the first sentence there are echoes, surely not unintentional. T.S. Eliot had remarked that "April is the cruellest month." The line echoes the beat and scan of the first line of the first poem in the true English language, Chaucer's *Canterbury Tales*: "Whan that Aprille with his shoures soote . . . ."

Now the educated reader will pick up these echoes, perhaps more; the common reader is likely to miss them. More generally, the educated reader will find many clues very quickly that we are dealing with satire. The common reader, for whom the book is really meant, may—indeed in my experience invariably does—take it all very literally. The press discusses whether we are in *Nineteen Eighty-Four* in 1984 and on the whole thinks the worse for Orwell that we are not.

For we now celebrate a nonevent: the year of the novel. My prime minister's speech-writers should have known better. On January 2, the *Times* reported:

> Mrs. Margaret Thatcher in a buoyant new year message to the Conservative Party yesterday said that George Orwell was wrong and she promised that 1984 would be a year of hope and liberty.

If he was writing a satire and not a prophecy, this remark is about as sensible as to say that Swift's view of the potential of human nature for both brutality and pettiness is false because Brobdingnag and Lilliput are not to be found on any admiralty charts, even of the South Atlantic. But the team would have got little help if they had called in that prince of general purpose intellectuals, Conor Cruise O'Brien. He said in the last issue of the *Observer* for 1983 that the book was not to be read as *generally* "anti-totalitarian": as Orwell himself had said:

> Anti-totalitarian is misleading because it is not specific enough. *Nineteen Eighty-Four* is not about some generalised form of oppression, which could be on the Left and could be on the Right. It is about as we shall see, something that could only be Communism as it developed in the Soviet Union. If [it] is even partially any kind of satire of our Western way of life, I'm a Chinaman.

As our Lord remarked to Pilate, "Thou sayest so."

Nineteen Eighty-Four is the most famous of Orwell's books, excepting perhaps his satire of 1945, *Animal Farm*; but the most misunderstood. What is essential to grasp is that, like *Animal Farm*, it is a satire, savage, powerful, even amusing (if one's stomach is strong), but not to be taken literally as a prophecy. If the press say, "Ah, it is not like he said it would be now," they are distancing it—either missing what it is a satire of or else trying to escape from it. A satire of what? Of many things, but primarily a satire of total power—how uncontrolled power always corrupts and proves inhuman. The original title was to have been, incidentally, "The Last Man in Europe." The actual title is simply the last two letters of 1948, the year in which he finished it, turned inside-out. It has no specific significance. We have been in "Nineteen Eighty-Four" for many years now (Orwell thought since 1938) and are likely (as the missiles multiply) to continue to be so.

The original dustjacket of the book both summarized the plot and gave a clue about the author's real intentions:

> 1984 is the year in which it happened. The world is divided into three great powers, Oceania, Eurasia and Eastasia, each perpetually at war with the others. Britain is part of Oceania and is known as Airstrip One. Throughout Oceania the Party rules by the agency of four Ministries, whose power is absolute—the Ministry of Peace which deals with war, the Ministry of Love which deals with law and order, the Ministry of Plenty which deals with scarcities, and the Ministry of Truth which deals with propaganda. "Newspeak" is the modern version of the English tongue ordained by the Party. It has given to the world such remarkable words as doublethink, thoughtcrime, plusgood and sexcrime ("love" in normal English). In every room throughout the land, including lavatories, a telescreen is installed that can never be switched off. . . .
>
> Against this nightmare background is played out the drama of Winston Smith, possibly the last man alive to rebel against the Party's rule and doctrines and to cling to a belief in the individual and in those precious human beliefs and values that are still strong today. . . .

And the summary ended by saying that George Orwell's *Animal Farm* had been hailed as a work by a "new Swift" and that this work was a satire too. It should be understood as a specifically Swiftian satire. Swift in *Gulliver's Travels* lashed the follies of mankind, almost as if he despaired of them: the darkness was part of a grim or black humor. And Swift worked by gross and savage caricature. We do not believe that there were giants in a place called Brobdingnag. But we do believe that mankind can be monstrously cruel and also careless. The power-hungry like tramping on us, or sometimes do it by accident because they do not notice us. We do not believe that there are dwarves in a place called Lilliput, but we do believe that mankind can be small, petty, pompous, and parochial. Orwell similarly worked by gross and savage caricature. He mocked the pretensions of those who would sacrifice liberty for our safety or welfare by saying that they—like the Inner Party interrogator, O'Brien, in the story—are only interested in "power for its own sake." Says O'Brien: "always there will be the intoxication of power, constantly increasing . . . the sensation of trampling on an enemy who is helpless. If you want a picture of the future, imagine a boot stamping on a human face—forever."

Orwell himself did not despair. When the first reviews of the book appeared in 1949, he was desperately ill with tuberculosis (dying in fact, but he did not know it), but his mind was clear and his strength enough to reply to some reviewers who saw the book both as totally pessimistic and as an implicit rejection of his well-known democratic socialism:

> It has been suggested by some of the reviewers of *Nineteen Eighty-Four* that it is the author's view that this, or something like it, is what will happen within the next forty years in the Western world. This is not correct. I think that, allowing for the book being after all a parody, something like *Nineteen Eighty-Four could* happen. . . .
>
> Specifically the danger lies in the structure imposed on Socialist and Liberal capitalist regimes alike by the necessity to prepare for total war with the USSR and the new weapons, of which, of course, the atom bomb is the most powerful and most publicised. But the danger lies also in the acceptance of a totalitarian attitude by intellectuals of all kinds.

It *could* happen, but need not. And it could happen here, Orwell was saying, and here meant England and the United States, as well as where it was already happening, in Stalin's empire, and where it had already happened, in Hitler's Europe. To Orwell, despotism was obviously despotism: the satire hardly needed to waste words on the obvious targets. But Orwell had always specialized in worrying about his own side, in warning that liberty is never safe enough in the hands of those who appear to possess it securely. He believed that "the price of liberty is eternal vigilance." So the book is a warning to the West, as well as a satire on the East. Satirically he shows three great powers in deadly rivalry becoming almost identical to each other out of the necessities of the cold war.

Now this has not happened. But he did not think that it would. He warned, however, against any tendencies whatever in that direction: he warned not merely against totalitarianism specifically but about power hunger in general. All his life he had been a rebel, the oddest mixture of an egalitarian and an individualist. He had won a scholarship to the most exclusive school in England, Eton, but refused to follow the old-fashioned curriculum and educated himself. He had served in the Imperial Police in Burma but grown to hate imperialism. After five years he returned to Europe, living among tramps and the very poor in both London and Paris for several years to see if our natives were treated by our upper classes as we had treated the native Burmese. On the whole, he thought they were. He wrote four novels in the 1930s, none of them very good though all interesting, but he wrote two extraordinary books describing his own experiences, *The Road to Wigan Pier*, about living among the unemployed, and *Homage to Catalonia*, about fighting in Spain against the fascists to save the Spanish Republic and discovering to his horror that the Communist Party was more concerned to purge its socialist and anarchist allies than to fight effectively against Franco. Early in the war he wrote a book, *The Lion and the Unicorn*, about the English national character, to try to convince his fellow socialists that there was no incompatibility between socialism and patriotism. He made many friends among wartime exiles from central and eastern Europe—such as Arthur Koestler and George Mikes. He liked the idea of a world of small nations and hated the rise of the great powerblocks, fearing not so much actual world war as the effect of permanent preparation for war. So while *Animal Farm* is obviously mainly mocking Stalin, it is a warning against power hunger in general and is a lament for the destruction of revolutionary idealism, not a warning against all and any revolution.

Animal Farm and *Nineteen Eighty-Four* are closely related works. The one tells the tale of revolution betrayed and the other of what would happen afterwards. And the moral, as he said in his press release, is "Don't let it happen; it depends on each one of us."

Perhaps *Nineteen Eighty-Four* was too ambitious for its own good. He packs several different satirical themes into it. Many students of Orwell think that *Animal Farm* is his finest work of art (leaving politics aside) and *Homage to Catalonia* his most original and difficult intellectual achievement. And mostly we remember him as a superb essayist and celebrant of popular culture, our last great popular novelist and educator, like Dickens and Wells. *Nineteen Eighty-Four* is only seemingly simple, in fact is complex and ambitious. I can see seven main satirical thrusts: (1) an attack on totalitarianism; (2) also an attack on power hunger in general, even in nontotalitarian countries; (3) an attack on the division of the world by the great powers at Yalta and Potsdam; (4) an attack on the intellectuals as a class for deserting for the relative safety of bureaucratic jobs their task of educating the people—he was almost obsessive in his distrust of intellectuals; (5) a defense of truth against the rewriting of history—as was happening all the time, not just in a future 1984; (6) a defense of plain language and plain speaking against official jargon and terminology; and (7) a savage attack on the mass media as the main device for controlling the proles not, remember, by terror and propaganda (that is for the Outer Party intellectuals and bureaucrats), but by debasement and trivialization. Remember what the whole range of the work of Julia's department was.

There was a whole chain of separate departments dealing with proletarian literature, music, drama, and entertainment generally. Here were produced rubbishy newspapers, containing almost nothing except sport, crime, and astrology, sensational five-cent novelettes, films oozing with sex, and sentimental songs which were composed entirely by mechanical means on a special kind of kaleidoscope called a versificator. There was even a whole section . . . engaged in producing the lowest kind of pornography.

And these views coincide so well with what Orwell himself was writing at that time. Consider this passage from "The Prevention of Literature" (1946):

It would probably not be beyond human ingenuity to write books by machinery. But a sort of mechanising process can already be seen at work in the film and radio, in publicity and propaganda and in the lower reaches of journalism. The Disney films, for instance, are produced by what is essentially a factory process, the work being done partly mechanically and partly by means of artists who have to subordinate their individual style. Radio features are commonly written by tired hacks to whom the subject and the manner of treatment are dictated beforehand. Even so, what they write is merely a kind of raw material to be chopped into shape by producers and censors. So also with the innumerable books and pamphlets commissioned by government departments.

Some people, nonetheless, claim that the book is morbid pessimism, not satire, because they find no alternative viewpoint. What about the proles?! Well, some say the proles are not delineated strongly enough. Remember what Winston Smith observes when he walks among the proles?

What mattered were individual relationships, and the completely helpless gesture, an embrace, a tear, a word spoken to a dying man, could have value in itself. The proles, it occurred to him, had remained in this condition. They were not loyal to a party or to a country or to an idea, they were loyal to one another. For the first time in his life he did not despise the proles or think of them as merely an inert force which would one day spring to life and regenerate the world. The proles had stayed human. They had not become hardened inside. They had held on to the primitive emotions, which he himself had to re-learn by conscious effort.

Could any encomium be stronger? Yet so many readers seem either to miss this and two or three similar passages, or else say—with more sense—that it is not stressed strongly enough to be taken seriously. We are back to the initial dilemma and ambiguity. To be taken seriously by whom? An intellectual reader, used to difficult novels, modern novels, futurist novels, trying to lump together everything from Henry James to Zamyatin and through Joyce, will read precisely and needs only a clear indication—as is given; but the common reader, whom Orwell loved and whom it behoves us all to support with all our powers, nonetheless does read more hastily. He may be likely to run over such passages and to judge the effect of a work by the rough balance of space and attention given to particular topics, rather than by those key passages which the satirist occasionally—very occasionally or else it spoils the form, structure, or even spoils a joke—uses to show us where he stands.

Yet it is a work of art, not a polemical tract—even if the work of art is somewhat overloaded by political elements, some of which are, however, speculative and analytical, not directly polemical at all. So as with any work of art, some will see more in it, some will see less, we will all read it differently. We all see what we want to see in any brilliant and complex satire that speaks to all mankind. But we misread it if we do not realize that it is a satire and not a despairing prophecy. Indeed, the intelligence of it should cheer us. Some of it should even make us laugh at things we still know. Laughter is a great enemy of tyranny. Historians and political scientists have concerned themselves with two modes of controlling absolute power: the first is to put power against power, checks and balances, defense, or even rebellion; the second is reason, persuasion—some might add prayer. But there is a third, much practiced by ordinary people under tyranny or even under free governments they cannot readily change; often ignored by historians and political scientists, or studied by students of literature only as a genre and not for its content or social force: satire. Orwell mocks the power-hungry and offers *Nineteen Eighty-Four* both as a mocking text and as a weapon in all such struggles.

Note: This essay drew on some material in George Orwell, *Nineteen Eighty-Four*, with a critical introduction and annotations by Bernard Crick (Oxford: Clarendon Press, 1984), which for copyright reasons is not available in the United States.

Orwell's Legacy
by Nathan A. Scott, Jr.

A few days after George Orwell's death on January 21, 1950, V. S. Pritchett in *The New Statesman and Nation* referred to him, in a great phrase, as "the wintry conscience of a generation." But this present symposium is merely one of innumerable signs that remind us that this was not just a role he enacted for his own generation; for his was, of course, a generation born in the very early years of this century, whereas he now remains—more than three decades after a lung hemorrhage in a Swiss sanatorium ended his long battle with tuberculosis—one of the great *directeurs de conscience* of our time. Indeed, it is, of all his work as a writer, most especially his two last books, *Animal Farm* and *Nineteen Eighty-Four*, that have become a permanent part of the moral history of the twentieth century. The day may come, though I strongly doubt it, when the idea of a totally controlled society run by a corps of self-elected *apparatchiks* will no longer be the fearful spectre that it is for the people who have lived through the past fifty years, but for as long as vast numbers of people anywhere in the world give their suffrage to the mystique of the absolute state Orwell's stern warnings about the demonry that modern totalitarianism entails will be unignorable.

And, moreover, the goading conscience that Orwell represents for us, most especially by way of *Nineteen Eighty-Four*, is surely something very wintry indeed. True, his purpose was to present in the terms of narrative a rendering of life in a totalitarian society that would have the effect of energizing a great effort of resistance. But so chilling is his vision of the "unfuture" that may be ahead that he very nearly subverts his primary intention by the intensity with which he sets forth the dread potentialities inherent in the mass societies of late modernity, potentialities that are made to appear so urgent as almost to invite the conclusion that their bursting into eventual actuality is well-nigh inevitable. A fashionable cliché says, to be sure, that *Nineteen Eighty-Four* is to be taken not as prophecy but as a baleful warning about the havoc that may be wrought by modern bureaucratic élites once they achieve despotic power. But, like many clichés, this gives us only a half-truth, as may be suggested by an article that Orwell published in *Partisan Review* in 1947, just two years before his account of life in Oceania appeared, an article entitled "Toward European Unity," where he was maintaining that three possibilities lay ahead of us: that (a) "the Americans will decide to use the atomic bomb while they have it and the Russians haven't," that (b) once the Soviet Union and other nations acquire the bomb, the great explosion will occur and the industrial centers of the world will be irreparably destroyed, and that (c) though the fear of the bomb may prove to be an effective constraint against its use, the world will come to be divided into "two or three vast super-states, unable to conquer one another and unable to be overthrown by any internal rebellion." The third possibility, he said, "seems to me the worst possibility of all," since these hierarchically organized super-states, "with a semi-divine caste at the top," would entail a "crushing out of liberty [that] would exceed anything that the world has yet seen."[1] And it was, of course, this possibility that he chose to hold up before us in *Nineteen Eighty-Four*. So the plain reader all across the world has not been wholly wrong over the past thirty-five years in taking this book to signify Orwell's having expected the future to be something very bad indeed.

But, fortunately, the act of imagination he performed in his book of 1949 with respect to the political future of the modern world has proved, just barely, to be more inspiriting than paralyzing, so that over these past decades the book has inured us to the habit of looking at this or that development in public life and interrogating it as to whether or not it augurs, in ever so slight a degree, the world that Orwell had foreseen as possibly having come to pass in the fifteenth year before the end of the twentieth century. And thus, as Prof. George Kateb has suggested, the book seems to stand a great chance of defeating its own predictions.[2]

Yet again and again in recent years the question has been raised, and sometimes with a good deal of inclination toward the negative view, as to whether or not the internal logic of *Nineteen Eighty-Four* provides a thoroughly cogent foundation for its ominous warnings and prognostications. Can it even be regarded as a novel at all, since the characters of the tale are so thinly and flatly drawn, making it therefore necessary, if the book is to be allowed any really suasive power, to hand over to Orwell a sort of blank check? And is it not the case that the despair which his testimony here bespeaks is so extreme as to be a kind of rabid sentimentality, expressing perhaps merely the fever of the death-bed on which much of the book was written? Or, again, more trenchantly, it is asked whether his analysis of the psychology of modern despots and of how power functions in totalitarian societies may not be seriously flawed.

The objection which is captiously taken by the literary mandarins to the presumed flatness and insubstantiality of the major personages in *Nineteen Eighty-Four* does not, of course, weigh significantly against Orwell's achievement: indeed, it is quite misconceived. True, apart from the vividness and complexity that Winston Smith and Julia begin to take on after the inception of their liaison, there is virtually no other evidence to be cited of the book's presenting human figures even approaching anything resembling multi-dimensionality. And by some of his critics this is held to be a centrally disabling failure of Orwell's narrative. But what is forgotten is that the whole logic of Oceania makes for a radical devaluation of the very idea of the autonomous self. Orwell's primary intention, as Irving Howe reminds us, is "to present the kind of world in which individuality has become obsolete and personality a crime."[3] And thus, given a situation in which the state has outlawed (as the totalitarian state tends ever more resolutely to do as it approaches its purest form) all the normal relations of society and, through its mechanisms of thought-control and surveillance, thoroughly suppressed the last vestiges of freedom, it is unreasonable to expect the landscape still to exhibit men and women who are activated by what Henry James called "the beautiful circuit . . . of . . . thought and . . . desire."[4]

Nor will it quite suffice to dismiss the pessimism of the book as being merely a token of the hopelessness induced by the desperate illness overhanging Orwell's last years. He did, of course, himself in a letter (February 4, 1949) to his friend Julian Symons say: "I ballsed it up rather, partly owing to being so ill while I was writing it."[5] But what he was surely intending to speak of was only his fear that the frequency with which his writing had had to be interrupted because of his infirmity and that the fatigue and discomfort that had had to be borne even when he was able to write may have resulted in the book's being less technically secure than might otherwise have been the case. Beyond this, however, it is unimaginable that Orwell would have had any inclination at all to accede to the notion that the fundamental judgments being expressed in *Nineteen Eighty-Four* about the crisis of modernity were grounded in nothing more than a kind of quasi-hysteria consequent upon his tuberculosis. And, indeed, such a view of his testimony is but perhaps the last evasion of the severity of the challenge which his book presents to the moral and political imagination of our time.

But what of Orwell's theory of power? It is on this, most assuredly, that the whole structure of *Nineteen Eighty-Four* rests, and that structure must collapse in the degree to which this theory fails in cogency.

The book presents, of course, a record of life at a late point in the history of the world, when it has become organized into but three vast super-states which are permanently at war with one another. This unending warfare is, however, carefully conducted in such a way as never to eventuate in any fundamental shift in the balance of power or in any kind of definitive victory or defeat, and thus it might seem to be merely a strange sort of barbaric sport. But it is something about which the ruling oligarchs are deadly serious, since they know that a state of constant war offers the best possible guarantee against unsettlement of their dominion. Moreover, perpetual war, in using up the goods that are produced in an industrial economy, keeps those goods out of the reach of the masses and thus condemns them to a life of deprivation that so stunts their minds and sensibilities as to disable any impulse there might otherwise be toward genuinely critical reflection. Which is to say that the oligarchs in the world of *Nineteen Eighty-Four* make no pretense of having any beneficent concern for the general human condition. At a late stage in the narrative, after the Thought Police have discovered Winston Smith to be guilty of what in Oceania is called "thoughtcrime," O'Brien, a member of the Inner Party who conducts the interrogation and torture, instructs Winston about how the system handles power: he says:

> The Party seeks power entirely for its own sake. We are not interested in the good of others; we are interested solely in power. Not wealth or luxury or long life or happiness: only power, pure power. . . . We are different from all the oligarchies of the past, in that we know what we are doing. All the others, even those who resembled ourselves, were cowards and hypocrites. . . . They pretended, perhaps they even believed, that they had seized power unwillingly and for a limited time, and that just round the corner there lay a paradise where human beings would be free and equal. We are not like that. We know that no one ever seizes power with the intention of relinquishing it. Power is not a means; it is an end. One does not establish a dictatorship in order to safeguard a revolution; one makes the revolution in order to establish the dictatorship. The object of persecution is persecution. The object of torture is torture. The object of power is power. . . . How does one man assert his power over another . . . ? . . . By making him suffer. Obedience is not enough. Unless he is suffering, how can you be sure that he is obeying your will and not his own? Power is in inflicting pain and humiliation. . . . Do you begin to see, then, what kind of world we are creating? It is the exact opposite of the stupid hedonistic Utopias that the old reformers imagined. A world of fear and treachery and torment, a world of trampling and being trampled upon, a world which will grow not less but *more* merciless as it refines itself. Progress in our world will be progress toward more pain. The old civilizations claimed that they were founded on love and justice. Ours is founded upon hatred. In our world there will be no emotions except fear, rage, triumph, and self-abasement. . . . If you want a picture of the future, imagine a boot stamping on a human face—forever.

Now it is O'Brien's disquisition on the nature of power that forms what is undoubtedly the central passage in Orwell's book. And it presents a fearsome lesson about how thoroughly the masters of a truly totalitarian society may be expected to radicalize such a traditional despotism as that for which the Grand Inquisitor in Dostoevsky's *The Brothers Karamazov* is an apologist. For the Grand Inquisitor justified the holding of absolute power on the ground that human beings are generally so weak and so timid that to relieve them of the burden of their freedom is to give them their great chance at happiness. Man in the large, in other words, cannot endure liberty and the open spaces of futurity, and so, says the Inquisitor, he "is tormented by no greater anxiety than to find some one quickly to whom he can hand over that gift of freedom with which . . . [he] is born." In short, the Caesars of the world, for all their iron-fisted tyrannousness, are really aiming at man's health and happiness. But with this kind of idealistic rationalization of absolute power the Inner Party of Oceania will not treat. Indeed, O'Brien does in effect disallow any role at all for ideology in a totalitarian regime, since, on his reckoning, it is terror alone that counts.

And it is surely a strength of Orwell's analysis that *Nineteen Eighty-Four* is guided by so clear a perception of how much a part of the critical essence of totalitarianism terror is. In this phase of his thought he was doubtless greatly influenced by what the Great Purges in the 1930s had disclosed of the inner workings of the Soviet system, but, whether one turns to the Bolshevik or the Nazi movement, it would seem that, once the demonic principle becomes regnant in the total state, it is indeed terror that in turn becomes the surrogate for law and the chief means for the execution of absolute power. For, as Hannah Arendt reminded us, total terror "substitutes for the boundaries and channels of communication between individual men a band of iron which holds them so tightly together that it is as though their plurality had disappeared into One Man of gigantic dimensions."[6] And, of course, this One Man is, says O'Brien, "infinitely malleable" by way of torture and propaganda and technology. As he says to Winston,

Already we are breaking down the habits of thought which have survived from before the Revolution. We have cut the links between child and parent, and between man and man, and between man and woman. No one dares trust a wife or a child or a friend any longer. But in the future there will be no wives and no friends. Children will be taken from their mothers at birth, as one takes eggs from a hen. The sex instinct will be eradicated. Procreation will be an annual formality like the renewal of a ration card. We shall abolish the orgasm. Our neurologists are at work upon it now. There will be no loyalty, except loyalty toward the Party. There will be no love, except the love of Big Brother.

But is it terror and sadism alone that prepare the way for and that knit together a totalitarian order? Orwell's insistence that they by themselves are sufficient must surely invite in some measure the response of simple incredulity, since it does so contradict our actual experience of the totalitarian mystique in this century. For even the most cynical of Hitler's minions wanted to validate their vision of the Third Reich and its destiny by appeal to doctrines of race and nature and to presumed laws of history. And, similarly, the thugs and gangsters in Stalin's employ had to live with something more than merely the naked lust for power: they required an elaborate doctrine of world-salvation and an elaborate eschatology not only for the suasion of the Russian multitudes but also, as one feels, for the justification to themselves of their own atrocities. And so it has generally tended to be in oligarchic societies: there is terror, yes, but terror rationalized by an ideology which offers consolations to both the masters and their victims—which makes one conclude that the world Orwell invented in *Nineteen Eighty-Four* is lacking a certain necessary linchpin.

Nor is this the only lacuna in Orwell's "argument," for Winston Smith's crucial question never quite gets answered. The entire apparatus of government in Oceania is in the hands of four ministries. First, there is the Ministry of Truth which, in its supervision of news and culture, specializes in the fabrication of lies. Then there is the Ministry of Peace, which conducts the unending wars. The Ministry of Love is in charge of law and order, having a special responsibility for the interrogation, torture, and "brainwashing" of political prisoners. Then, finally, there is the Ministry of Plenty, which, in bearing responsibility for economic affairs, has the job of organizing scarcity. Winston, of course, as a minor functionary in the Ministry of Truth, knows how this whole system works; yet the question which he cannot answer but which he ponders endlessly is the question as to why his world is organized as it is and what its ultimate cause might be considered to be. As he one day confides to his diary, "I understand HOW: I do not understand WHY."

Now, had it not so largely evaded this great bullying question, Orwell's book might well have proved to be even more powerful than it is. Orwell himself was, of course, not without some understanding of what lies at the root of the totalitarian phenomenon. In, for example, a letter to an American acquaintance (June 16, 1949), the labor-unionist Francis Henson, who was at the time the education director of the United Automobile Workers, Orwell said of *Nineteen Eighty-Four*: "My recent novel is NOT intended as an attack on Socialism or on the British Labour Party (of which I am a supporter) but as a show-up of the perversions to which a centralised economy is liable and which have already been partly realised in Communism and Fascism. I do not believe that the kind of society I describe necessarily *will* arrive, but I believe . . . that something resembling it *could* arrive. . . . The scene of the book is laid in Britain in order to emphasise that the English-speaking races are not innately better than anyone else and that totalitarianism, *if not fought against*, could triumph anywhere."[7]

This is, one feels, an authorial dictum that deserves to be remembered, in part because it lays to rest two common misinterpretations of Orwell's intention. On the one hand, many have supposed that the aggressions of his satire were directed at the Britain of Clement Attlee and Sir Stafford Cripps, at the gray, fusty dispensation over which the Labour government of the forties presided, and at some ultimate bankruptcy which he foresaw for English socialism. Then, on the other hand, a more common tendency has been to take *Nineteen Eighty-Four* as principally an attack on the kind of police state represented by the Soviet Union. But, as Orwell's letter to Francis Henson suggests, his polemic was primarily directed elsewhere, for, as he says, the book was calculated to expose "the perversions to which a centralised economy is liable." And we ought to take this term *economy* in its broadest sense, not as designating merely a system of producing and distributing material goods but as a term speaking of the mode whereby all the affairs and interests of a people are ordered and administered. In other words, the economy or dispensation that Orwell feared and that he took to be everywhere looming on the modern scene was one in which all of life is organized and regimented by a bureaucratic elite. Which is to say that, at bottom, the prompting cause of his great apprehension was the emergence of what Karl Mannheim called "the planned society."[8] Here, as he felt, is what the whole drift of the modern world is leading towards. And this is why he considered everybody to be in the same boat—those in Britain and France and the United States as well as those in Russia. For all of us dwell now in that late time in which modern society is everywhere becoming mass society and in which the available apparatus of communications and social technique permits whichever minority happens to be in power to rule with absolute power. And thus, given the hybris which this situation engenders, the ravenous desire to expand for expansion's sake and to politicize every nook and cranny of the human order, it is with an almost inexorable logic that a "centralised economy" moves toward the total state.

The Oceania of *Nineteen Eighty-Four* does undoubtedly in many ways present a mirror-image of Stalin's Russia, but what needs to be stressed is that, for Orwell, the totalitarian state of our time is itself but an image of the future that may be awaiting us all, since it is not so much the controversion as the final development of that whole process involving the centralization (and politicization) of the human economy that has been at work in the West ever since the time of Danton and Robespierre and Saint-Just. So Prof. Robert Nisbet is surely right in suggesting that the book whose lengthened shadow falls across Orwell's book is Burke's *Reflections on the Revolution in France*.[9] And, surprising as it may be to remark the fact, Orwell's thought has, indeed, many significant affinities with the outlook of such thinkers as Ortega and Berdyaev and Marcel and Jaspers. For, like these and numerous other conservative ideologues of the modern period, Orwell knew that the Jacobins controlling a centralized economy are prepared, once they can claim the endorsement of the general will (which is "infinitely malleable"), to do *anything* in behalf of *their* conceptions of Reason and Virtue, and he knew that, just here, is the seedbed of the totalitarian state. This is not to say, however, that neo-conservatives on the American scene of the present time can properly claim him, as they have sometimes lately done, to be of their own tribe. For Orwell was a democratic socialist, and, were he now among us, his boundless compassion for the underdog, for the poor and the powerless and the unfortunate, would make him very impatient indeed with the kind of sour meanspiritedness that is so deeply a part of our new conservative ideologies. But he held his own political allegiance with a wonderfully inspiring skepticism, and, like Burke and de Tocqueville and Ortega and Hannah Arendt, he knew that, given the pressure of unpropitious circumstances, one of the important dramas of the modern period may be expected to move from mass democracy and a cult of leadership to the obliteration of traditional values and institutions and on to the militarization of society and the monolithic, total state.

It needs to be remarked, however, that, though the Grand Inquisitor's view of political power is in effect set aside in *Nineteen Eighty-Four*, the logic of Orwell's thought does nevertheless keep us within the universe of *The Brothers Karamazov*, since that whole tragic drama leading from a "centralised economy" to the total state can never play itself out unless Ivan Karamazov's conclusion, that "everything is permitted," has in some measure become the reigning principle of a culture. Everything must seem possible, and everything must seem permitted, and all that was God's must henceforth seem at the disposal of Caesar: it is the pervasion of a people's life by such presumptions as these that forms the necessary soil for the growth of the kind of order represented by Oceania. The sacred must have gone into eclipse, and the world must have fallen under the sway of the profane, of what the historian of religion Mircea Eliade calls the *désacralisé*. The question, in other words, that Winston Smith commits to his diary when he writes, "I understand HOW: I do not understand WHY," is a question which cannot begin to be answered apart from some exploration of the profound moral and religious crisis that forms the environing matrix within which the disease of totalitarianism becomes a contagion. But into this range of things Orwell does not venture. For, deeply inured as he was to the habits of thought engendered by the traditions of English empiricism, he mistrusted anything savoring of abstraction, and, as he faced into the great issues of public life, it was his habit to rely on little more than such commonsensical notions as those of decency and liberty and fairness and responsibility—which did not, of course, offer him either a lexicon or a body of ideas adequate to the large themes with which he was engaged. Had he been submitted to formal interrogation, he no doubt might well have admitted, with perhaps either some impatience or reluctance, that, within the terms of Camus' *L'Homme révolté*, "metaphysical rebellion" does indeed probably precede "historical rebellion." But he had no inclination to inquire into what the former may entail, and it was just this lack of interest in the "metaphysical" that kept him from producing in *Nineteen Eighty-Four* a richer and more cogent book.

Max Weber once remarked of himself, "I am . . . absolutely unmusical in religious matters." But to recall the profundity of Weber's empirical studies of religion and the staleness of Orwell's occasional animadversions on religion (as simply an affair of fairy-tales, as so much hocus-pocus about "the hereafter," etc.) is surely to feel immediately that Weber's confession might far more appropriately have come from Orwell. Indeed, it is his failure of mind and imagination in this region of things that not only prevents his being able fully to reckon with the question that overwhelms Winston Smith but that also keeps him from even recognizing the final irony of his own narrative in *Nineteen Eighty-Four*. Rather curiously in Winston's last session with O'Brien, as he is being furiously catechized, with the dial being turned up by O'Brien to increase his pain when the wrong answers are given, at a certain point O'Brien says: "Do you believe in God, Winston?" It is a question somewhat strange because anything resembling religious nurture or instruction has for so long been so systematically extirpated by the rulers of Oceania that one cannot but wonder how O'Brien might have expected Winston to have at hand any ready answer at all. But Winston's answer is promptly given and he says, "No." It is an awkward moment, and Orwell immediately moves on in his exposition of the scene, for he is not himself equipped to explore what kind of transcendent reality it might be in which Winston *could* believe. And, of course, the whole episode culminates at last in Winston's caving in. After it is discovered that he and Julia in their secret liaison have violated one of the cardinal rules laid down for members of the Party, great pains are taken with (as O'Brien calls it) his "re-integration"—which involves savage beatings and ingeniously arranged tortures that are administered in "Room 101," a high, windowless cell somewhere in the Ministry of Love. And, as a result of this discipline, Winston is eventually reduced to a listless, shuffling ghost who is convinced that the Party is right, that the so-called laws of nature are nonsense, that freedom is slavery, that two and two make five. In short, victory is won, and he at last truly loves Big Brother. But is it really physical torture by which he is undone? Is it not rather the case that his collapse is, at bottom, induced by nothing more than his being without any principle whatsoever wherewith, even in his utter vulnerability before his inquisitors, he might be enabled to say, however feebly and faintly, "No, do with me what you will, but you shall not have my soul, or at least that which I have recovered of it through what Julia and I have had together." All he can inwardly summon is hatred of his oppressors, though even this is finally snuffed out—but, as Christopher Small shrewdly remarks, "hate is not opposed to the Party's theology at all but is the main point of its doctrine."[10] And, amongst the multifarious data Orwell's narrative presents, Winston's being unable to respond with anything but a simple negative when O'Brien asks him if he believes in God is surely the saddest of all. But the authorial intelligence controlling the invented world of *Nineteen Eighty-Four* evinces no adequate appreciation of its terrible pathos.

Yet, however much the partialities of Orwell's vision may have delimited what might have been the far greater range of his final book, it remains one of the preeminent testaments of this century, a work whose genius and power make one feel insolent indeed in passing any kind of judgment upon it at all. Happily, the dreadful possibility it holds forth has not materialized, though there are, of course, those who will not acknowledge this to be the case. And perhaps nothing more attests to the perduring strength of Orwell's book than the degree to which it manages to escape the kind of banality to which it would be reduced by those who, wherever they turn on the Western scene, are prepared eagerly, and almost delightedly, to point to myriad signs of ours having already become (as they say) an "Orwellian" world. Any infelicity or vulgarity in the discourse of our politicians, or any obfuscating maladroitness in the jargon of our bureaucrats, is immediately pounced on as betokening the invasion of the public order by the "Newspeak" of the age. The various banks of computerized data held by business and governmental institutions and the uses of electronic surveillance by our law enforcement agencies are declared to be the irrefutable evidence of how helplessly we languish under the dominion of "Big Brother." And of the making of such analogies there is no end, especially amongst those Americans whose hostility toward American society prompts them to mangle any and every fact for the sake of establishing that American social and political culture is at the very least as morally ambiguous as the Soviet system. But all this is the sheerest buncombe. For when one looks either at the American scene or at Western society in the large, it would hardly seem, for all the manifest imperfections, that the freedom and privacy of individual persons are severely threatened by anything like the hypertrophied state depicted in *Nineteen Eighty-Four*. Indeed, it may well be that a case could be advanced in support of the proposition that, if the social and political structures guaranteeing freedom are by anything threatened, it is not so much by the Leviathan as by a certain anarchic antinomianism that insidiously gnaws away at the fabric of inherited codes and norms.

The misconception of Orwell's book as primarily an essay in "futurology" must yield, in other words, a large measure of disappointment, if the contemporary scene is viewed with any kind of sanity at all, for that scene offers no confirmation of the narrative taken as simple prophecy. But, of course, though he would seem, when one recalls his *Partisan Review* essay of 1947 ("Toward European Unity"), to have been somewhat inclined towards a baleful view of the immediate prospect he felt himself to be facing, Orwell's most fundamental intention was to warn. And, on this level, his testimony remains as pungent and relevant as it was when we were all first captivated by *Nineteen Eighty-Four* thirty-five years ago. For vigilance in the defense of democratic norms is as necessary today as at any previous point in the last fifty years. True, totalitarianism in its German form of the 1930s and 40s is dead; but, in its Russian form, though it has undergone some measure (as Max Weber would say) of routinization that may have entailed a certain dampening of the ardor of the old revolutionary messianism, it yet retains a great lust for empire—of which we are bound to be reminded when we consider the present situation of eastern Europe and the persistently thrusting adventurism of the Soviets in many widely separated parts of the world. And, beyond the spheres of the Soviet Union and the People's Republic of China, there is surely no scarcity on the contemporary scene of tyrants presiding over authoritarian regimes whose brutality in the handling of power would appear indeed to be modeled on the classic examples provided by German fascism and Russian Communism. Nor is the distinction very persuasive which American neo-conservatives are fond of making between totalitarian and authoritarian regimes. They ask us to regard authoritarian systems as somehow less malign than the genuine totalitarian article, since they do not create large refugee populations or "violate internalized values and habits" but "leave in place existing allocations of wealth . . . [and] power," "worship traditional gods," and "do not disturb the habitual rhythms of work . . . [and] patterns of family and personal relations."[11] So, as it is argued, traditional autocracies represent a "systemic" difference from the revolutionary autocracies of totalitarianism. But this is a difference too subtle to be appreciated by the victims of the Vietnamese, Korean, Iranian, Libyan, Nicaraguan, Philippine, Haitian, and Cuban oligarchies (to mention only a few)—all of which are more or less distant heirs of totalitarian regimes. And Orwell's hatred of a boot being trampled anywhere on a human face would surely have led him to be more than a little impatient with any nice distinctions between totalitarian and authoritarian systems: no, as he would have said, under whatever form tyranny is tyranny, and by no scholastic rhetoric can the obliteration of freedom in the one case be made less odious and obscene than in the other: no, as the author of *Nineteen Eighty-Four* would say, only under the compulsions of doublethink can "Big Brother" in one region of the universe be thought to be more benign than "Big Brother" in some other region of the world. Indeed, as he would remind us in his unpretentious and commonsensical way, if two and two under all circumstances make four, then, under all circumstances, "Big Brother" remains "Big Brother."

So the warning that was being sounded in his book of thirty-five years ago remains something absolute and still terribly urgent. For the survival of free societies is as much dependent today as ever before on their resisting the kind of radical evil represented by totalitarianism in all its various forms, the kind of evil that sponsors political systems that would (in Hannah Arendt's phrase) "make men superfluous."[12] And the great challenge in this regard that forms Orwell's principal legacy deserves, therefore, to be heeded with undiminished seriousness, even now in this year of our Lord 1984.

Notes

1. George Orwell, "Toward European Unity," in *Partisan Review*, vol. 14, no. 4 (July–August, 1947), 346–47.
2. George Kateb, "The Road to *1984*," in *The Political Science Quarterly*, vol. 81, no. 4 (December 1966), 577.
3. Irving Howe, *Politics and the Novel* (New York: Meridian Books, 1957), 237.
4. Henry James, *The Art of the Novel: Critical Prefaces* (New York: Charles Scribner's Sons, 1934), 32.
5. *The Collected Essays, Journalism and Letters of George Orwell*, 4 vols., ed. by Sonia Orwell and Ian Angus (New York: Harcourt Brace Jovanovich [A Harvest Book], 1968), 4:475.
6. Hannah Arendt, *The Origins of Totalitarianism* (New York: World Publishing Co. [A Meridian Book], 1958), 465–66.
7. *The Collected Essays*, vol. 4, 502.
8. See Karl Mannheim, *Diagnosis of Our Time* (New York: Oxford University Press, 1944), passim.
9. See Robert Nisbet, "*1984* and the Conservative Imagination," in *1984 Revisited: Totalitarianism in Our Century*, ed. by Irving Howe (New York: Harper and Row, 1983), 181.
10. Christopher Small, *The Road to Miniluv: George Orwell, the State, and God* (Pittsburgh: University of Pittsburgh Press, 1975), 207.
11. Jeane J. Kirkpatrick, *Dictatorships and Double Standards: Rationalism and Reason in Politics* (New York and Washington, D.C.: American Enterprise Institute and Simon & Schuster, 1982), 49–50.
12. Hannah Arendt, op. cit., 457.

Discussion

The first speaker from the floor, CHUCK BERGER, addressed Mr. CRICK with "a few points in rebuttal." Having lived in the U.S.S.R. under Stalin for a year, with the freedom to observe as an American citizen, Mr. BERGER finds *Nineteen Eighty-Four* neither parody nor satire, but rather "a desperate warning by a desperate man who saw what I saw there: . . . constant terror, condemnations, and punishments by Big Brother, and the utter futility to complain or correct." The observations he made from his point of view as an eyewitness included: a government bureaucracy dominated by a small group who have arrogated authority; a "bunch of rules, regulations, restrictions, and obligations imposed on the proles under threat of punishment"; an abstraction immune to attack because "you cannot 'get' an abstraction." "As of today, I can guarantee you that [Big Brother] is in Russia and it is exactly as Mr. [Orwell] wrote." Mr. CRICK countered that the questioner and other "obsessional [anti-]Stalinists" who "only see Stalin in *Nineteen Eighty-Four*" will "read almost any text in the same kind of way" and went on to describe Orwell as "attacking a much wider range of phenomena than simply Stalinists. . . . Orwell attacks all kinds of power, abuse of power, petty power, and great power. . . . So I just totally disagree with your reading of *Nineteen Eighty-Four*." Later in this session Mr. CRICK said "it's absolutely clear that *Nineteen Eighty-Four*, however odd it may seem to some, was viewed by Orwell, in his stubborn old way, as an attack on all kinds of hierarchy, including socialist, but as also including conservative or fascist or any other type."

From the floor it was asked if, taking the message of the book as a warning of the loss of our liberties, there are any guideposts in *Nineteen Eighty-Four* that indicate when we have reached the danger point. Mr. SCOTT said that while he knows of nothing in Orwell that offers a yardstick wherewith to know when "the beast is about to pounce," he suspects that Orwell's sense of history told him "we'd been in a kind of zone of danger for a long time," since, for Orwell, modern industrial society's drift toward centralization of economy, of life and culture, "betokens danger ahead." A follow-up question was addressed to Mr. CRICK whether he knows of a better solution to incursions on private rights than the Constitution of the United States. Mr. CRICK finds it an "admirable document" insofar as it "can be amended and can move with the times and doesn't stay in 1787," and speculated that if one could ask Orwell "when you can tell when things are going to the bad, I think he would give the old Jeffersonian—Tocquevillian answer: 'when private citizens cease to care for public concerns.'" While Mr. CRICK granted that Orwell had a distrust of the centralized state in common with today's conservatives—("I can see why some of the radical right like to snatch his body")—he nevertheless insisted that "*Nineteen Eighty-Four* does not represent a repudiation of Orwell's socialism," and that Orwell would not be a "neo-conservative" if he were alive today. Mr. SCOTT added that, given Orwell's sympathy for the underdog, the poor, the unfortunate, in contrast to the neo-conservatives' "sour meanspiritedness," he rubs his eyes "with disbelief as neo-conservatives of the present time undertake . . . to claim Orwell as their own." Mr. CRICK took the position that "people misread the satire" who read *Nineteen Eighty-Four* as a satire on Soviet totalitarianism, on the issue of the paternalistic centralized government, since Orwell tells us "precisely three times in the novel" that it's the Outer Party, the intellectuals, and not the proles, who are terrorized by the Inner Party; that "the Secret Police rarely go among the proles, there are few telescreens in their homes: they are controlled by pornographic newspapers, triviality, sport, astrology, five-cent novelettes, prostitution, drugs, and booze. . . . Orwell sees the state as providing them in order to trivialize the people. I think he was full of rage . . . that every liberal in the nineteenth century had thought that the effects of compulsory education and the free franchise would be some kind of enlightened citizen body like the ideal picture of the New England town meetings, and what do we get? We get the mass press, the city, an indifferent mass population. I think that's what [Orwell is] really gunning at."

Mr. CRICK took up the "puzzling question as to how much formal philosophy Orwell knew." Nobody really knows, although Orwell knew Bertrand Russell and was a personal friend of A. J. Ayer, whether he read "the difficult books" or whether he "came up with these epistemological paradoxes out of a fantastic imagination. . . . I think it's at least credible that Orwell had that kind of imagination on a very commonsense basis; but it's also plausible that he might have had a direct connection with [Karl] Popper's articles."

Both Mr. CRICK and Mr. SCOTT were asked to comment on how Orwell's neologisms such as doublethink, newspeak, and Big Brother have become a part of our language and what their effect has been. Mr. SCOTT commented that while the neologisms have come into common parlance, we should bear in mind that their violent crudity, as "pieces of language themselves," should be thought of in the narrative's context, in relation to Airstrip One. Mr. CRICK observed that Orwell had a "perfectly insufferable contempt" for the academic activity of inventing language, "was attacking that all the time," and that "prolefeed" is an important invention of Orwell's to show the kind of abuses he warned against. In fact, Mr. CRICK recently heard a reputable, working English journalist use the expression "cynically, self-deprecatingly, almost despairingly: 'Two-thirds of this bloody newspaper, Bern, is just prolefeed.' "

From the floor, a questioner asked if Orwell was considered by the English government, or by any body of readers, to be a traitor for writing, in *Nineteen Eighty-Four*, not so much a warning as a blueprint. Mr. SCOTT said that the book was initially reviewed in the Communist press with animus, that the old Left Book Club did not "offer him three cheers," and that the steadily dwindling circle of English Stalinists viewed the book with "some biliousness," but that no one else on the English scene would have been inclined to see

Orwell as a traitor. Mr. CRICK said it is not a blueprint but plainly a complex parody, chiefly mocking James Burnham's idea that power can be held for its own sake but also showing in O'Brien that "people who hold too much power go crazy, actually end up holding absurd views." Mr. CRICK said Orwell is "swinging around rather wildly with a lot of blows at once," hitting the Catholic Church, idealism, and also certain types of metaphysical philosophy.

After replying "yes" to a question whether Orwell was a socialist at the end of his life, Mr. CRICK was asked about the apparent discrepancy between Orwell's valuing individual autonomy and being a socialist who ipso facto cannot exist "without a social setting, without rules and regulations to which he must conform." Mr. CRICK began his response by calling Orwell "a perfectly ordinary bloke who paid his taxes and obeyed normal social conventions and wished to see social change in a socialist direction," who, however, laid himself open to misreading by the very nature of satire. A prime difficulty of satire is that "you have to assume that readers know where you stand," and Orwell made a mistake with *Nineteen Eighty-Four* which had also happened with *Animal Farm*: "I think Orwell was a bit of an old socialist romantic in the . . . Western European sense, who thought that the Russian Revolution was a good thing, to simplify it, but it had been betrayed by Stalin and Lenin." Thus, *Animal Farm*, "textually and in the author's intention, was a satire on the revolution betrayed, not a satire on revolutions in general." However, a lot of reviewers—not only but mainly in the United States—said that *Animal Farm* was "an attack on revolution, socialism, communism, and anything else going in general." Mr. CRICK here took Orwell to task for imprudence in not "making clearer, either in the story or the presentation" of *Nineteen Eighty-Four*, where he stood, after "that bad experience" of *Animal Farm*'s critical reception. With satire, Mr. CRICK stated, which is not "like a normal mode of literature, you can't take it just within the text, and you probably haven't got enough within the text" to make fully clear the implications of the text.

Mr. KAZIN disagreed with Mr. CRICK's idea that O'Brien's views are a parody, but holds that they are a "blueprint" of the extraordinary contempt for truth, not only in tyrannies but in democracies like our own. Mr. KAZIN went on to say that Orwell "was really concerned about . . . the crippling of truth by modern states." Mr. KAZIN gave three examples of leaders he finds lying "to a degree which is absolutely unbelievable"; in the United States, our leaders lied before, during, and after the Vietnam war; in the U.S.S.R., "a country which notoriously has a great respect for science, and in which many scientists have worked very brilliantly," there was "an amazing abdication of scientific truth during the Stalin period"; and in Nazi Germany, there was "talk about a Jewish physics as opposed to real German physics." Mr. KAZIN said that O'Brien exemplifies the actual, "active belief [on the part of] many governments today that their control over people is enough to make them say that two and two equal five, and the people can't say anything about it." Mr. KAZIN, finding O'Brien one of the most serious parts of the novel, challenges

Mr. Crick on O'Brien-as-parody, because O'Brien "is a blueprint of what people really think in many governments today."

Mr. CRICK answered that O'Brien is parodic specifically when he says the Party could change the laws of geology, change the laws of nature, etc., and that in O'Brien, Orwell "means two things: a parody on the corrupting effect of total power, unchallenged power; and also, a kind of salutary tale. I agree with Dr. Kazin absolutely [about] what happens if you habitually tell untruths in politics: you end up believing your own lies."

A member of the audience with an interest in social and developmental psychology observed that perhaps humanity at this juncture is stuck at a developmental level where we have to divide the world into all-good / all-bad, right and wrong, perfect and imperfect, prior to reaching a more evolved, humanistic level. In giving Orwell's book a psychological interpretation, the questioner asked why we need authoritarian leaders, why we create omnipotence in our heroes and our villains, and suggested that perhaps we need to destroy God in order to destroy our tremendous need for authoritarianism. Mr. HECHT replied, "Nietzsche had a crack at it already."

Mr. DONOGHUE agreed with the burden of Mr. Kazin's concern for truth-telling in politics but is doubtful that Kazin is on strong ground in calling Orwell to witness in its favor and pointed to the distinction Orwell makes in his essay "Writers and Leviathan" between the citizen and the writer. In that essay, written in March 1948, Orwell says that the citizen should do nearly any work he's called upon to do for his political party or at a time of war in favor of "the grandest cause," but he should not write for it or engage in propaganda on its behalf. For the writer, whatever he is called upon to do as a citizen, his writing should always be "the product of the saner self that stands aside, records the things that are done, and admits their necessity but refuses to be deceived as to their true nature."

Mr. KAZIN's response was that Orwell worried about conscience and felt "it was very important to know that you were lying." He mentioned Hannah Arendt's remark that in his novel Orwell "recognized that one must never lie to oneself but it's all right to lie to other people." In addition, Mr. KAZIN told of hearing Ezra Pound's broadcasts in Italy and of a rumor nowadays that "a lot of that stuff was manufactured by the F.B.I., that Pound never said these things. My first reaction to this [rumor] is to say, 'My God, what kind of a world are we living in?' The second one is to say, 'That's the kind of a world we are living in.' " We are living in a world in which more and more people whom Mr. KAZIN knows are beginning to say, " 'Well, if they say [Auschwitz] never occurred, perhaps they're right.' " Later in the session, a member of the audience commented that General Eisenhower after D-Day took it upon himself to go through every nook and cranny of some of the concentration camps, precisely because he felt it "possible that in the future people would doubt they had ever existed."

Mr. CRICK said that although Orwell was a perfectly realistic person who realized that in politics you sometimes "couldn't tell the whole truth, and sometimes venal lies were told by a party, or sometimes you tell genial nonsense," Orwell had a "tougher moral realism" that made him draw the citizen/writer distinction. Alfred Kazin's mention of Pound should remind us that "the moral and the aesthetic dualism were both fundamental to Orwell. . . . Of Pound he could say, 'Anti-Semite, loathsome fascist, great poet.' ·" When Orwell says the writer must always stand back as a critic, Mr. CRICK believes "he's using *writer* in a very extended sense . . . trying to say to . . . all journalists and communicators, 'You should have the dignity of the writer and not of the slave. You shouldn't be one of Julia's machines.' "

A member of the audience asked for agreement from Mr. Crick that Orwell, far from specifying any particular ideology at all, was getting at our own vulnerability to what Jefferson called "any form of tyranny over the mind of man." The questioner said that "we can't rely on institutions to protect us, because they can be dissolved in Newspeak; we can't rely on character, because it will be dissolved in Room 101; [and added, isn't] Orwell saying what Walt Kelly expressed as, 'We have met the enemy, and he is us.' "

Mr. CRICK responded that both Walt Kelly and George Orwell are saying, "Don't get into that kind of situation to start with," but Orwell is not "making a comfortable liberal individualistic point that you can always heroically resist even in the darkest regime. . . . Orwell is grimly aware that people had been . . . and could be broken completely in certain kinds of social situations." Then Mr. CRICK wanted "to swing to the other tack and say . . . 'please, please don't think this is only about Stalin.' . . . It is about . . . not merely a future model but of the well-known old happening in Europe in the 1930s." Orwell, having looked Hitler and Stalin "squarely in the eyes," in the very midst of the post-war celebrations was wondering "whether it was really all over, whether the battlefield had really settled the social and ideological and moral default."

CHRISTOPHER HITCHENS from the floor had "one small correction, one agreement, and one dissent" for Mr. Crick. The correction: regarding the Bollingen award to Pound, Orwell actually said that if the judges thought Pound's poetry to have the greatest literary merit, no objection to his fascist ideas should impede the award, although Orwell added that he himself thought the poetry greatly overrated; "anti-Semite, lousy fascist, great poet" was not quite the triad he achieved. The agreement: Mr. HITCHENS found Mr. Crick's remarks about Swift and satire very fertile, and related the story about the bishop who, preaching a sermon against *Gulliver's Travels*, said he had read every book of it and did not believe a word. A suggestion made by "a mutual enemy of ours, Paul Johnson," is that irony should be set in a special typeface, so that we may recognize it. The dissent: Mr. Crick had "not quite crushed" the questioner on the matter of O'Brien and the blueprint. Mr. HITCHENS said that, although it was not known to Orwell, modern totalitarian states have invoked the supernatural (in the case of North Korea and China); have attributed supernatural abilities to their "god-like" leaders; and have attempted to say that the laws of nature and biology can be suspended in favor of the dictates of such people ("Lysenko was obviously the best-known case"). Mr. HITCHENS emphasized that what Orwell would notice was not that the Russian scientists and academicians, who had to agree with Lysenko, agreed with him; but that people in free countries, notably France and Great Britain, people like J. D. Bernal, voluntarily agreed that the laws of nature had been suspended in Stalin's favor. Mr. HITCHENS observed, in concluding this salient contribution to the meaning of *Nineteen Eighty-Four* in 1984 and beyond, that the appalling picture Orwell draws of the crushing ability to make people obey is rarely missing from Orwell criticism and evaluation. What *is* often missing is attention to his portrayal of the will to obedience generated by the people themselves, their readiness to be servile, their hope that one can get by without thinking for oneself.

Concluding the session and the conference, Mr. SCOTT replied, to audience questions, that Orwell was neither religious in any organized religious sense nor did he "permit himself any kind of dogmatical atheism." As to the hereafter and supernatural beings, Mr. SCOTT answered that Orwell dismissed religion "as a lot of hocus-pocus. . . . He was just tone-deaf, religiously . . . and I don't recall anywhere any measured and well-modulated statements of Orwell about religion. He was just impatient with it."

Mr. CRICK thinks that, for Orwell, sociability—"fraternity, treating other people as equals"—justified morality, and he quoted from "Orwell's second essay on Koestler . . . a very strange and interesting paragraph," which closes, "The real problem is how to restore the religious attitude while accepting death as final. Men can only be happy when they do not assume that the object of life is happiness."

Mr. SCOTT answered a questioner who wondered where Orwell's morality was fixed, thus: "He in no way supposed, ever, that religious presuppositions offered any kind of necessary warranty for moral sanctions. Morality he conceived to be something quite, quite independent of [religion]."

For the Library of Congress, Mr. HECHT adjourned the conference.

Bibliography: A Selected List of References

Bibliography:
A Selected List of References

Compiled by Marguerite D. Bloxom
General Reading Rooms Division

The following entries, representing books and periodical articles, were selected to provide a balanced view of George Orwell and his work, particularly his novel, *Nineteen Eighty-Four*. Works selected are primarily in English, although a few recent foreign language items are included.

THE MAN AND THE AUTHOR
General Works and Biographies

Besançon, Alain.
  Orwell in our time / Alain Besançon ; translated by Rebecca Penrose. — In *Survey : a journal of East and West studies.* — Vol. 28 (spring 1984) ; p. 190-197.
                                                                                                     DK1 .S549
General discussion of several of Orwell's works and their themes.

Byrne, Katharine.
  A different-looking Orwell. — In *Commonweal.* — Vol. 110 (Mar. 11, 1983) ; p. 147-151.
                                                                                                     AP2 .C6897

Campbell, Beatrix.
  Wigan Pier and beyond. — In *New statesman* — Vol. 106 (Dec. 16/23 1983) ; p. 23-24.
                                                                                                     AP4 .N64
In 1984 both Right and Left are going to claim Orwell's prophecies as theirs. Both would agree with his depiction of the working class as corrupt and unconscious.

Charpier, Jacques.
  George Orwell, a "Tory anarchist." — In *Unesco courier.* — 37th year (Jan. 1984) ; p. 4-7 : ill.
                                                                                                     AS4.U8 A14

Biographical summary of his life and work.

Crick, Bernard R.
George Orwell, a life / Bernard Crick. — 1st American ed. — Boston : Little, Brown, c1980. — xxx, 473 p., [16] p. of plates : ill.
PR6029.R8 Z627 1980
Includes bibliographic references and index.

George Orwell. — In *L'Arc.* — *[no.]* 94 (1984) ; p. 3-105.
[PQ2 .A7 no. 94]
Contents: Le Démon de George Orwell / Jean-Jacques Courtine — Une oeuvre plurielle / Catherine Rihoit — La Lettre et le chiffre / Michael Viel — Comment j'ai tué un éléphant / George Orwell — Le Chemin de Marrakech ou comment Orwell devint anti-impérialiste / Gilbert Bonifas — Préface à la Vache enragée / Panait Istrati — Hommage à la Catalogne, l'expérience du corps / Jean-Claude Larrat — George Orwell et la question de la langue / Jean-Jacques Courtine — G. Orwell derrière la porte : langage secret, langage obscène / Catherine Rihoit — L'injonction à l'impassibilite dans 1984 / Claudine Haroche — Romanesque et politique dans *1984* / François Brune — George Orwell et les fonctionnaires de la vérité / Roger Raby — *1984* et la poétique de la parodie / Jon R. Snyder.

[George Orwell]. — In *Modern fiction studies.* — Vol. 21 (spring 1975) ; p. 3-136.
PS379 .M55
Entire issue devoted to George Orwell.
Contents: Orwell as an old Etonian / Martin Green — Dance to a creepy minuet : Orwell's *Burmese Days*, precursor of *Animal Farm* / John V. Knapp — Orwell's *A Clergyman's Daughter* : the flight from history / Richard I. Smyer — In dubious battle : George Orwell and the victory of the money-god / Nicholas Guild — George Orwell's *Coming Up for Air* / Jeffrey Meyers — Orwell and antisemitism : toward *1984* / Melvyn New — Zamyatin's *We* and the genesis of *1984* / James Connors — Some recent books on Orwell : an essay review / Richard J. Voorhees — George Orwell : a selected checklist / Jeffrey Meyers.

[George Orwell]. — In *Quinzaine litteraire.* — *(Du 16 au 29 Fev. 1984)* ; p. 5-12 : ill.
micro 06131 AP
A collection in French of short articles, reviews, and translations.

[George Orwell]. — In *World review.* — new series, Vol. 16 (June 1950) ; p. 3-61 : port.
AP4 .W84
Special issue devoted to George Orwell with portions of his unpublished notebooks.
Partial contents: Editorial / Stefan Schimanski — George Orwell / Bertrand Russell — A Writer's life / T. R. Fyvel — The Unpublished notebooks of George Orwell — REVALUATIONS: *Burmese Days* / Malcolm Muggeridge ; *The Road to Wigan Pier* / John Beavan ; *Homage to Catalonia* / Stephen Spender ; *Animal Farm* / Tom Hopkinson ; *1984* / Herbert Read — A footnote about *1984* / Aldous Huxley.

George Orwell's America / [collected and introduced by] Richard F. Snow. — In *American heritage.* — Vol. 35 (Feb./Mar. 1984) ; p. 65-80 : ill.
E171 .A43
Selections from Orwell's work revealing his impressions of things American, particularly American writers and language. Included are essays about Henry Miller, "American words," American troops in England, American magazines, Harriet Beecher Stowe, Bret Harte, and Jack London.

Hunter, Lynette.
George Orwell, the search for a voice / Lynette Hunter. — Milton Keynes, England : Open University Press, 1984. — 242 p.
Bibliography: p. 227-229.
PR6029.R8 Z7115 1984
Examines Orwell's writing style in detail, noting his rhetorical techniques, concern with language, and narrative perspective.

Jones, Landon Y.
George Orwell — In *People weekly.* — Vol. 21 (Jan. 9, 1984) ; p. 38, 41-42, 45. : ill.
AP2 .P417
Includes a brief illustrated column on Richard Blair, Orwell's adopted son, and his life today.

Kalechofsky, Roberta.
George Orwell. — New York : F. Ungar Pub. Co., [1973]. — ix, 149 p. — (Modern literature monographs).
Bibliography: p. [137]-141.
PR6029.R8 Z714

Kirk, Russell.
George Orwell's despair. — In *Intercollegiate review.* — Vol. 5 (fall 1968) ; p. 21-25.
AP2 .I64
Although Orwell professed sympathy with laborers and the lower classes, his awareness of himself as "distinctly middle-class" prevented him from becoming a true revolutionary. He yearned for an earlier, easier time remote from social problems.

Kubal, David L.
Freud, Orwell, and the bourgeois interior / David Kubal. — In *Yale review.* — Vol. 67 (Mar. 1978) ; p. 389-403.
AP2 .Y2
Observes similarities in the thought and backgrounds of the two men, particularly their respect for the Victorian anchor of the home.

Lewis, Wyndham, 1882-1957.
Orwell, or Two and two make four. — In his *The writer and the absolute.* — London : Methuen, [1952]. — p. 153-194.
PN151 .L45
A biographical summary based on an uncritical reading of the autobiographical portions of Orwell's work is followed by less than reverent criticism of his novels and essays.

Meyers, Jeffrey.
Orwell's painful childhood. — In *Ariel.* — Vol. 3 (Jan. 1972) ; p. 54-61.
PR1 .R352
Bibliographic footnotes.
Boarding school days were a source of suffering and guilt that influenced Orwell's later work.

Oxley, B. T.
George Orwell / [by] B. T. Oxley. — London : Evans Bros., 1967. — 144 p., 4 plates. — (Literature in perspective)
PR6029.R8 Z75

Bibliography : p. 138-143.

Pour Orwell — In *Esprit : changer la culture et la politique.* — *[New series, no. 85]* *(Jan. 1984) ; p. 13-38.*
AP20 .E78

Special section devoted to Orwell.
Contents: [Introduction] / Jeanyves Guérin — La Logique de la lucidité / Gil Delanno — La Théorie des catastrophes graduelles / George Orwell — La Mémoire du denier homme et la resistance / Georges Lavau — Nous et la bombe atomique / George Orwell — Le combat contre les monstres / Jacques Darras.

Rees, Richard, Sir.
George Orwell : fugitive from the camp of victory / Richard Rees ; with a pref. by Harry T. Moore. — Carbondale : Southern Illinois University Press, [1962]. — 151 p. — (Crosscurrents : modern critiques)
PR6029.R8 Z77 1962

"Bibliographical Note on Orwell's Books and Essays": p. [147-148].

Rodden, John.
Orwell and Catholicism : the religious fellow traveler. — In *Commonweal.* — *Vol. 111 (Sept. 7., 1984) ; p. 466-470.*
AP2 .C6897

Despite Orwell's frequently voiced attacks against religion, especially Catholicism, religious writers continue to try to claim him as their own. "The paradoxically warm response of Catholics to Orwell illumines the larger pattern of Orwell's reception on the right . . . and illustrates how observers project selected aspects of a thinker's work onto the author's whole corpus."

Stansky, Peter.
Orwell, the transformation / Peter Stansky and William Abrahams. — 1st American ed. — New York : Knopf, 1980. — 302 p., [2] leaves of plates : ill.
PR6029.R8 Z7898 1980

Includes bibliographic references and index.
The second half of Orwell's biography, begun with *The Unknown Orwell.*

Stansky, Peter.
The unknown Orwell / [by] Peter Stansky and William Abrahams. — [1st ed.]. — New York : Knopf, 1972. — xx, 316, xiii p. : ill.
PR6029.R8 Z79

Includes bibliographic references.

Thomas, Edward Morley.
Orwell / [by] Edward M. Thomas. — New York : Barnes & Noble, [1968, c1965]. — 114 p. — (Writers and critics)
PR6029.R8 Z8 1968

Bibliography: p. [111]-114.

Thompson, John.
Orwell's London / John Thompson ; photographs by Philippa Scoones. — 1st American ed. — New York : Schocken Books, 1985, c1984.
Not yet in LC collection.

Trilling, Lionel.
George Orwell and the politics of truth : portrait of the intellectual as a man of virtue. — In *Commentary*. — *Vol. 13 (Mar. 1952) ; p. 218-227.*
DS101 .C63

Voorhees, Richard Joseph.
George Orwell : rebellion and responsibility / Richard J. Voorhees. — In *South Atlantic quarterly*. — *Vol. 53 (Oct. 1954) ; p. 556-565.*
AP2 .S75

Williams, Raymond.
George Orwell : a collection of critical essays / [comp. by] Raymond Williams. — Englewood Cliffs, N.J. : Prentice-Hall, [1974]. — viii, 182 p. — (A Spectrum book. Twentieth century views)
PR6029.R8 Z865
Bibliography: p. 181-182.
Contents: Introduction / Raymond Williams — Orwell and the lower-middle-class novel / Terry Eagleton — Introduction to *The Road to Wigan Pier* / Richard Hoggart — Observation and imagination in Orwell / Raymond Williams — George Orwell and the politics of truth / Lionel Trilling — Inside which whale? / E. P. Thompson — George Orwell as a writer of polemic / John Wain — Orwell as satirist / Stephen J. Greenblatt — *1984*, the mysticism of cruelty / Isaac Deutscher — Orwell's post-war prophecy / Jenni Calder.

Williams, Raymond.
Orwell. — [London] : Fontana, [1971]. — 95 p. — (Fontana modern masters).
PR6029.R8 Z87
Bibliography: p. 95.

Woodcock, George.
The crystal spirit : a study of George Orwell. — [1st ed.]. — Boston : Little, Brown, [1966]. — vii, 366 p.
PR6029.R8 Z9
"A Selective Bibliography of Orwell's Works": p. [357]-358.

Woodcock, George.
George Orwell, 19th century liberal. — In *Politics*. — *Vol. 3 (Nov. 1946) ; p. 384-388.*
JK1 .P74
In *The Crystal Spirit*, Woodcock notes that this was the first critical essay published about George Orwell.

Zehr, David Morgan.
Orwell and the proles : revolutionary or middle class voyeur? — In *Centennial review*. — *Vol. 27 (winter 1983) ; p. 30-40.*
AS30 .C45
Observes Orwell's "disturbing ambivalence" toward the working class. Although he walked among lower classes he remained an observer, not an "actual comrade." He identified with the values of the class, but not with the class itself.

Personal Recollections

Buddicom, Jacintha Laura May.
Eric and us : a remembrance of George Orwell / Jacintha Buddicom. — London : Frewin, 1974. — xxi, 169 p., [16] p. of plates : ill., facsims., geneal. tables, map, ports.

PR6029.R8 Z59

Dunn, Avril.
My Brother, George Orwell. — In *Twentieth century.* — *Vol. 169 (Mar. 1961)* ; *p. 255-261.*

AP4 .N7

Fen, Elisaveta.
George Orwell's first wife. — In *Twentieth century.* — *Vol. 168 (Aug. 1960)* ; *p. [115]-126.*

AP4 .N7

Fyvel, T. R. (Tosco R.)
George Orwell, a personal memoir / T. R. Fyvel. — New York : Macmillan, c1982. — x, 221 p., [8] p. of plates : ports.

PR6029.R8 Z636 1982

Includes bibliographic references and index.

Heppenstall, Rayner.
Four absentees. — London : Barrie and Rockliff, 1960. — 206 p.

PR6015.E56 Z5

Descriptions of his relationship with Orwell appear throughout the book. Some of his material was published first in *Twentieth Century*, Vol. 57, Apr.-May 1955.

Hollis, Christopher.
A study of George Orwell : the man and his works. — Chicago : H. Regnery Co., 1956. — 212 p.

PR6029.R8 Z68

"Eton": p. 11-25.

Orwell remembered / [edited by] Audrey Coppard & Bernard Crick. — New York : Facts on File, c1984. — 287 p.

PR6029.R8 Z745 1984

"This book arose from the BBC's Arena programme, Orwell Remembered, which was televised in three parts early in 1984." The interviews have been supplemented by published material and by selections from the BBC archives, "notably a Third Programme feature of 2 November 1960 which Rayner Heppenstall, a close friend of Orwell's, produced."

Powell, Anthony.
George Orwell : a memoir. — In *Atlantic monthly.* — *Vol. 220 (Oct. 1967)* ; *p. 62-68.*

AP2 .A8

Potts, Paul.
Don Quixote on a bicycle. — In *London magazine.* — *Vol. 4 (Mar. 1957)* ; *p. 39-47.*

PR1 .L65

Warburg, Fredric, 1898—
All authors are equal : the publishing life of Fredric Warburg, 1936-1971. — New York : St. Martin's Press, 1974, c1973. — xii, 310 p., [3] leaves of plates : ill.

Z325.W29 A298 1974

"Animal Farm": p. 35-[58] ; "1984": p. 92-[120].
Includes bibliographic references and index.

The World of George Orwell / edited by Miriam Gross. — London : Weidenfeld and Nicolson, 1971. — [10], 182 p., 64 plates : ill., facsims., ports.

PR6029.R8 Z92

While some of the following accounts may not be strictly personal, the effect of the book is to give an impression of Orwell as he was known to friends and associates. Contents: The Young Eric / Jacintha Buddicom — Schooldays / Francis Hope — George Orwell and Burma / Maung Htin Aung — Imperial attitudes / John Gross — A Note on Orwell's Paris / Richard Mayne — Orwell's slumming / Dan Jacobson — Along the road to Wigan Pier / Ian Hamilton — Orwell and the Spanish Civil War / Raymond Carr — In the thirties / John Wain — Orwell at the BBC / William Empson — The critic of popular culture / John Coleman — The Years at Tribune / T. R. Fyvel — Orwell and communism / Edward Crankshaw — Memories of George Orwell / Michael Meyer — From *Animal Farm* to *Nineteen Eighty-Four* / Matthew Hodgart — Orwell's reputation / David Pryce-Jones — Arguments against Orwell / D. A. N. Jones — A Knight of the woeful countenance / Malcolm Muggeridge.

Orwell's Political and Social Views

Beadle, Gordon B.
George Orwell and the death of God. — In *Colorado quarterly*. — Vol. 23 (summer 1974) ; p. 51-63.

AP2. C6634

Orwell, like Dickens, was a moral rather than an ideological critic of society. He urged social reform via Christian principles in a post-Christian world.

Beadle, Gordon B.
George Orwell and the neoconservatives / Gordon Beadle. — In *Dissent*. — Vol. 31 (winter 1984) ; p. 71-76.

HX1 .D58

Vigorously denies that Orwell would ever have associated himself ideologically with conservatives. In his demands for social justice he was consistently a left-wing socialist and revolutionary.

Birrell, T. A.
Is integrity enough? A study of George Orwell. — In *Dublin review*. — Vol. 224 (third quarter, 1950) ; p. 49-65.

AP4 .D8

While rejecting formal religions, Orwell sought for society a religious attitude characterized by decency and morality. But he spent his energy in the quest of a fruitless ideal.

Connors, James.
"Who dies if England lives?" : Christianity and the moral vision of George Orwell. — In *The Secular mind : transformations of faith in modern Europe : essays presented to Franklin L. Baumer, Randolph W. Townsend Professor of History, Yale*

University / edited by W. Warren Wagar. — New York : Holmes & Meier, 1982. — p. 169-196.

BL2747.8 .S33 1982

Bibliographic references included in "Notes" (p. 193-196).
Orwell denied the truth of Christianity but retained a belief that mankind needed morality and common decency. A religion of humanity and a sense of community could provide secular inspiration for these virtues.

Glicksberg, Charles Irving.
George Orwell and the morality of politics. — In his *The literature of commitment* / Charles I. Glicksberg. — Lewisburg [Pa.] : Bucknell University Press, c1976. — p. 289-318.

PN51 .G53

Bibliographic footnotes.
Portions of this essay were published in the *Arizona Quarterly*, Vol. 10, Autumn 1954, p. 234-245.

Ingle, Stephen.
Note on Orwellism / S. Ingle. — In *Political studies.* — Vol. 28 (Dec. 1980) ; p. 592-598.

JA1 .P63

Offers an interpretation of Orwell's socialism based on a study of several of his books.

Johnstone, Richard.
George Orwell. — In his *The will to believe : novelists of the nineteen-thirties* / Richard Johnstone. — Oxford ; New York : Oxford University Press, 1982. — p. 119-129.

PR888.B44 J64 1982

Bibliographic references included in "Notes" (p. 129).
Orwell was equally suspicious of Catholicism and communism as solutions for society's problems. His attempt to view the world realistically only deepened his pessimism.

Kubal, David L.
Outside the whale : George Orwell's art and politics / [by] David L. Kubal. — Notre Dame [Ind.] : University of Notre Dame Press, [1972]. — xvii, 169 p.

PR6029.R8 Z715

Bibliography: p. 159-163.

Lutman, Stephen.
Orwell's patriotism. — In *Journal of contemporary history.* — Vol. 2 (Apr. 1967) ; p. 149-158.

D410 .J66

Orwell perceived patriotism as an emotion, often unconsciously generated, that was most frequently observed in the lower classes. Although love of country could be a powerful motivator, it could not be manipulated intellectually.

McNamara, James.
Waiting for 1984 : on Orwell and evil / by James McNamara & Dennis J. O'Keefe. — In *Encounter [London].* — Vol. 59 (Dec. 1982) ; p. 43-48.

AP4 .E44

Bibliographic footnotes.
Examines Orwell's theories of social organization noting aspects of control, stratifica-

tion, knowledge, and language, "all of these grouped round a highly original perception of evil as a political category."

Patai, Daphne.
The Orwell mystique : a study in male ideology / Daphne Patai. — Amherst : University of Massachusetts Press, 1984. — x, 334 p.
Bibliography: p. [269]-317.
PR6029.R8 Z753 1984

Rossi, John.
Why the Left hates Orwell. — In *Intercollegiate review.* — *Vol. 17 (spring/summer 1982) ; p. 97-105.*
AP2 .I64
He exposed Leftist hypocrisy and "made them ashamed of their cliches."

Rowse, A. L.
Contradictions of George Orwell. — In *Contemporary review.* — *Vol. 241 (Oct. 1982) ; p. 186-194.*
AP4 .C7
Charges that Orwell lacked a knowledge of history and an understanding of politics, both of which are necessary to prognostication of the future.

Walsh, James.
George Orwell. — In *Marxist quarterly.* — *Vol. 3 (Jan. 1956) ; p. 25-39.*
AP4 .M34
A response written by Peter Thirlby and entitled "Orwell as a Liberal," was published in the October issue p. 239-247.

Watson, George.
Orwell and the spectrum of European politics. — In *Journal of European studies.* — *Vol. 1 (Sept. 1971) ; p. 191-197.*
D1 .J58
As a political journalist Orwell saw that the differences between Left and Right were often more illusory than factual.

Wykes, David.
Orwell in the trenches. — In *Virginia quarterly review.* — *Vol. 59 (summer 1983) ; p. 415-435.*
AP2 .V76
Examines Orwell's perceptions of warfare, particularly as revealed in *Homage to Catalonia*.

Zwerdling, Alex.
Orwell and the Left / Alex Zwerdling. — New Haven : Yale University Press, 1974. — xii, 215 p.
PR6029.R8 Z97
Includes bibliographic references and index.

Orwell's Writing: Criticism and Interpretation

Alldritt, Keith.
The making of George Orwell : an essay in literary history. — London : Edward Arnold, 1969. — [7], 181 p.
PR6029.R8 Z57

Beadle, Gordon B.
George Orwell's literary studies of poverty in England. — In *Twentieth century literature.* — *Vol. 24 (summer 1978) ; p. 188-201.*
PN2 .T8
Bibliographic footnotes.
Orwell's preoccupation with poverty was rooted in his sense of guilt and fired by his indignation at socialist intellectuals who viewed the misery of poverty as an abstraction.

Calder, Jenni.
Chronicles of conscience : a study of George Orwell and Arthur Koestler. — London : Secker & Warburg, 1968. — 303 p.
PR6029.R8 Z6
Bibliography: p. [291]-294.

Crompton, Donald.
False maps of the world — George Orwell's autobiographical writings and the early novels. — In *Critical quarterly.* — *Vol. 16 (summer 1974) ; p. 149-169.*
AP4 .C887
The past, romantically recalled as a time of security and decency, was important to Orwell. His recollections often colored his interpretations of the present.

Dutsher, Alan.
Orwell and the crisis of responsibility. — In *Contemporary issues.* — *Vol. 8 (Aug./Sept. 1956) ; p. 308-316.*
AP4 .C685
Questions the inevitability of the success of a totalitarian system as well as the assumption that achieving power is the ultimate human satisfaction.

Fiderer, Gerald.
Masochism as literary strategy : Orwell's psychological novels. — In *Literature and psychology.* — *Vol. 20 (no. 1, 1970) ; p. 3-21.*
PN49 .L5
Bibliographic footnotes.
Notes Orwell's many mentions of whippings, canings, and beatings in his autobiographical notes and suggests that his five major novels can be understood through the dynamics of masochism.

George Orwell : the critical heritage / edited by Jeffrey Meyers. — London ; Boston : Routledge & K. Paul, 1975. — xiv, 392 p. — (The Critical heritage series)
PR6029.R8 Z64
Bibliography: p. 382.
Examines 108 reviews of Orwell's work noting their themes and characteristics.

Greenblatt, Stephen Jay.
George Orwell. — In his *Three modern satirists : Waugh, Orwell, and Huxley.* — New Haven : Yale University Press, 1965. — *p. 37-73.*
PR937 .G7
Bibliographic footnotes.
Analyzes Orwell's background and experiences to show how they contributed to the bitterness evident in his writing.

Hammond, J. R. (John R.)
A George Orwell companion : a guide to the novels, documentaries, and essays /

J. R. Hammond. — New York : St. Martin's Press, 1982. — xii, 278 p., [4] leaves of plates : ill.

Bibliography: p. 266-274.

PR6029.R8 Z663 1982

Hodge, Bob.
Orwellian linguistics / Bob Hodge and Roger Fowler. — In *Language and control* / Roger Fowler . . . [et al.]. — London ; Boston : Routledge & K. Paul, 1979. — p. 6-25.

P120.V37 L3

Hunter, Jefferson.
Orwell's prose : discovery, communion, separation. — In *Sewanee review.* — Vol. 87 (summer 1979) ; p. 436-454.

AP2 .S5

Jurgensen, Jean-Daniel.
Orwell, ou, La route de 1984 / Jean-Daniel Jurgensen. — Paris : Editions R. Laffont, c1983. — 208 p.

PR6029.R8 Z712 1983

Includes bibliographical references.

Justman, Stewart.
Orwell's plain style — In *University of Toronto quarterly.* — Vol. 53 (winter 1983/ 84) ; p. 195-203.

AP5 .U55

In Orwell's writing statements of fact and judgments are barely distinguishable. He distrusted abstract language and yet his writing is full of ideas, plainly put.

Knapp, John V.
Orwell's fiction : funny but not vulgar. — In *Modern fiction studies.* — Vol. 27 (summer 1981) ; p. 294-301.

PS379 .M55

Bibliographic footnotes.
The usual interpretation of Orwell's novels as realistic may have deterred readers from seeing instances when his satire "borders on the ludicrous."

Lang, Berel.
The politics and art of decency : Orwell's medium. — In *South Atlantic quarterly.* — Vol. 75 (autumn 1976) ; p. 424-433.

AP2 .S75

Lee, Robert A.
Orwell's fiction / [by] Robert A. Lee. — Notre Dame [Ind.] : University of Notre Dame Press, [1969]. — xvii, 188 p.

PR6029.R8 Z72

Bibliography: p. 179-183.

Leys, Simon.
Orwell, ou, L'horreur de la politique / Simon Leys. — Paris : Hermann, c1984. — 74 p. — (Collection Savoir)
Not yet in LC collection.
Includes bibliographical references.

Lief, Ruth Ann.
Homage to Oceania : the prophetic vision of George Orwell. — [Columbus] : Ohio State University Press, [1969]. — viii, 162 p.
                                                                PR6029.R8 Z73
Bibliographic references included in "Notes" (p. [147]-158).

Mander, John.
Orwell in the sixties. — **In his** *The writer and commitment*. — London : Secker & Warburg, [1961]. — p. 71-102.
                                                                PR471 .M27 1961

Meyers, Jeffrey.
A reader's guide to George Orwell / Jeffrey Meyers. — London : Thames & Hudson, [1975]. — 192 p.
                                                                PR6029.R8 Z737
"Notes on the Text": p. [163]-180 — Bibliography: p. [181]-185.

Møller, Per Stig.
Orwells hab og frygt / Per Stig Møller. — Copenhagen : Gyldendal, c1983. — 180 p.
                                                                PR6029.R8 Z7373 1983

Quintana, Ricardo.
George Orwell : the satiric resolution. — **In** *Wisconsin studies in contemporary literature*. — Vol. 2 (winter 1961) ; p. 31-38.
                                                                PN2 .W55
Through satire Orwell attempted to keep good and evil in balance in his writing.

Raskin, Jonah.
George Orwell and the big cannibal critics. — **In** *Monthly review*. — Vol. 35 (May 1983) ; p. 40-45.
                                                                HX1 .M67
Observes that the critics have used Orwell for their own purposes and exploited him for their own aims.

Sandison, Alan.
The last man in Europe : an essay on George Orwell. — [London ; New York] : Macmillan, [1974]. — 203 p.
                                                                PR6029.R8 Z78 1974
Bibliography: p. [191]-201.

Shapiro, Marjorie.
George Orwell's criticism. — **In** *Connecticut review*. — Vol. 6 (Apr. 1973) ; p. 70-75.
                                                                AS30 .C62
Bibliographic footnotes.
Orwell interpreted literature from an author's viewpoint, seeking to define the message in the work. Aesthetic judgments, he believed, should be separated, in so far as possible, from one's acceptance of the message.

Slater, Ian.
Orwell : the road to airstrip one / Ian Slater. — 1st ed. — New York : Norton, c1985.
Not yet in LC collection.

Smyer, Richard I.
Primal dream and primal crime :   Orwell's development as a psychological novelist / Richard I. Smyer. — Columbia : University of Missouri Press, 1979. — viii, 187 p.

Bibliography: p. 176–182.

PR6029.R8 Z789

Swingewood, Alan.
Orwell, socialism, and the novel. — In *Laurenson, Diana.* — *The sociology of literature* / [by] Diana Laurenson and Alan Swingewood. — London : MacGibbon and Kee, 1972. — p. 249–275.

Bibliographic footnotes.

PN51 .L35

Voorhees, Richard Joseph.
George Orwell as critic / Richard J. Voorhees. — In *Prairie schooner.* — *Vol. 28 (summer 1954)* ; p. 105–112.

AP2 .P85285

Warncke, Wayne.
George Orwell's critical approach to literature. — In *Southern humanities review.* — *Vol. 2 (fall 1968)* ; p. 484–498.

AS36.A86 A35

Bibliographic references included in "Notes" (p. 497–498).
In his book reviews Orwell examined the author's sincerity, point of view, responsibility to the reader, and sources. The critic's task, he thought, was to clarify the world view represented in the work at hand.

West, Anthony.
George Orwell. — In his *Principles and persuasions : the literary essays of Anthony West.* — [1st ed.]. — New York : Harcourt Brace, [1957]. — p. 164–176.

PN511 .W44

Orwell's pessimism was rooted in his unhappy childhood.

Willison, Ian R.
Orwell's bad good books / Ian Willison. — In *Twentieth century.* — *Vol. 157 (Apr. 1955)* ; p. 354–366.

AP4 .N7

The typical Orwell hero borders on mediocrity and lacks the resources to control his own life.

Workman, Gillian.
Orwell criticism. — In *Ariel.* — *Vol. 3 (Jan. 1972)* ; p. 62–73.

PR1 .R352

Bibliographic footnotes.
Earlier critics based their observations on a knowledge of Orwell's life and character. Later ones, who had not known him, sought to locate his work in a literary context.

Bibliographies

McDowell, M. Jennifer.
George Orwell : bibliographical addenda. — In *Bulletin of bibliography.* — *Vol. 23 (Jan./Apr. 1963)* ; p. 224–229. — *Vol. 24 (May/Aug. 1963)* ; p. 19–24. — *(Sept./Dec. 1963)* ; p. 36–40.

Z1007 .B94

Supplements the bibliography by Zeke and White and includes film reviews by Orwell, letters of reply to Orwell's articles and reviews, chapters in books, obituaries, and portraits.

Meyers, Jeffrey.
George Orwell : an annotated bibliography of criticism / Jeffrey and Valerie Meyers. — New York : Garland Pub., 1977. — ix, 132 p., [5] leaves of plates : ill. — (Garland reference library of the humanities ; v. 54)

Z8647 .M485

Based on two checklists previously published by the compiler, the bibliography summarizes "books, articles and important reviews in English, French, Italian, Spanish, German, Dutch, Norwegian and Japanese."

Willison, Ian R.
George Orwell : bibliographical addenda / I. R. Willison and Ian Angus. — In *Bulletin of bibliography.* — Vol. 24 (Sept./Dec. 1965) ; p. 180–187.

Z1007 .B94

Zeke, Zoltan G.
George Orwell : a selected bibliography / Zoltan G. Zeke and William White. — [Boston] : Boston Linotype Print, 1962. — 12 p.

Z8647 .Z45

"Reprinted from the *Bulletin of Bibliography* (The Faxon Co.) Vol. 23, no. 5, May-August 1961; no. 6, September-December 1961; and no. 7, January-April 1962." A list of books, essays, and reviews by George Orwell and essays and reviews by Eric Blair as well as a checklist of items about Orwell including books, chapters in books, periodical articles, and reviews.

NINETEEN EIGHTY-FOUR, A NOVEL

A film version, "1984" was produced by Columbia Studios in 1956. It starred Edmond O'Brien as Winston with Jan Sterling as Julia and Michael Redgrave as O'Brien. A copy of the film is in the Library's collections in the custody of the Motion Picture and Television Reading Room. Also in the collections are stills, press book, and lobby cards for the film.

Special Editions of the Novel

Nineteen eighty-four, a novel / by George Orwell — [1st ed.]. — London : Secker & Warburg, 1949, — 312 p.

PZ3 .O793Ni2

Nineteen eighty-four / George Orwell ; with a critical introduction and annotations by Bernard Crick. — Oxford : Clarendon Press ; New York : Oxford University Press, 1984.
Not yet in LC collection.

Nineteen eighty-four : the facsimile of the extant manuscript / George Orwell ; edited by Peter Davison ; with a preface by Daniel G. Siegel. — San Diego : Harcourt

Brace Jovanovich ; Weston, Mass. : M & S Press, 1984 — xix, 381 p. : facsims.

PR6029.R8 N49 1984c

Orwell's Nineteen eighty-four : text, sources, criticism / edited by Irving Howe. — 2nd ed. — New York : Harcourt Brace Jovanovich, 1982. — x, 450 p. — (Harbrace sourcebooks)

PR6029.R8 N49 1982

Rev. ed. of Nineteen eighty-four. c1963.
Includes passages from similar works (or "sources") and from Orwell's essays and letters. Also represented are selections from early reviews of the novel, essays of literary criticism about *Nineteen Eighty-Four*, and essays on totalitarianism.

Criticism of the Novel

Aldiss, Brian W.
The downward journey : Orwell's 1984. — In *Extrapolation*. — *Vol. 25 (spring 1984) ; p. 5–12.*

PN3448.S4 E59

Explores the role of opposites and paradoxes in Orwell's novel. In 1948 the work appeared to be a grim prophecy; in 1984 it calls to mind parallel instances from reality of "political bullying," wars and totalitarianism, revolution, hedonism, and shortages. "We see the novel's transformation through time: from prophecy of the future to a parable of our worldly existence, 1948–84."

Ashe, Geoffrey.
Second thoughts on *Nineteen Eighty-Four*. — In *Month*. — *new series, Vol. 4 (Nov. 1950) ; p. 285–300.*

AP4 .M65

Barnsley, John H.
"The last man in Europe" : a comment on George Orwell's *1984*. — In *Contemporary review*. — *Vol. 239 (July 1981) ; p. 30–34.*

AP4 .C7

Barr, Alan.
The paradise behind "1984." — In *English miscellany*. — *Vol. 19 (1968) ; p. 197–203.*

PR13 .E45

Orwell employs Christian symbology and details in a fairly consistent pattern throughout the work. The Party is rigid and authoritarian as is the Church. Big Brother appears as savior, and Goldstein is a loudly reviled Satan.

Bolton, W. F. (Whitney French).
The language of 1984 : Orwell's English and ours / W. F. Bolton. — Knoxville : University of Tennessee Press, [1984]. — 252 p.

PR6029.R8 Z588 1984

Bibliographical references included in "Notes" (p. 225–235). — Bibliography: p. 236–245.
A study of changes in the English language since World War II that takes George Orwell as its starting point "concentrating on changes in English and the attitudes towards it as they diverge from his." To claim this perspective Bolton attempts first to clarify Orwell's language theory and practice. The book thus "sets out both a view of Orwell and a view of our present-day language."

Clarke, I. F.
1984 and not *Nineteen Eighty-Four*. — In *Futures (England)*. — *Vol. 16 (Feb. 1984) ; p. 4-17.*

HB3730 .F8

Locates Orwell's work in its literary traditions starting with *Gulliver's Travels* and comparing it with other futuristic works including *We* and *Brave New World*. Clarke notes that such works reflect postwar anxieties about the future: "the great destructive dystopias of modern times are signs of the constant search for balance in the world."

Crick, Bernard.
Nineteen Eighty-Four : satire or prophecy? — In *Dutch quarterly review of Anglo-American letters*. — *Vol. 13 (no. 2, 1983) ; p. 90-102.*

PE9 .D87

"An expanded and more detailed version of this argument will appear in an introduction to an edition of *Nineteen Eighty-Four* to be published by Clarendon Press, Oxford, in 1984."
Comes down on the side of satire, noting that the author's positive values "emerge on the contrary of what he is attacking." Orwell seeks a fairer world than the disgusting one he portrays.

Currie, Robert.
The "big truth" in *Nineteen Eighty-Four*. — In *Essays in criticism*. — *Vol. 34 (Jan. 1984) ; p. 56-69.*

PR1 .E75

The novel is basically about madness, particularly schizophrenia, with overtones of homosexuality.

Edrich, Emanuel.
George Orwell and the satire in horror. — In *Texas studies in literature and language*. — *Vol. 4 (spring 1962) ; p. 96-108.*

AS30 .T4

Bibliographic footnotes.

Elsbree, Langdon.
The structured nightmare of *1984*. — In *Twentieth century literature*. — *Vol. 5 (Oct. 1959) ; p. 135-141.*

PN2 .T8

Points to Orwell's use of changing imagery as Winston moves from reverie to tortured nightmare in an inescapable sequence of distorted events. The novel's characters move in the dreamlike state of helpless individuals.

Feder, Lillian.
Selfhood, language and reality : George Orwell's *Nineteen Eighty-Four*. — In *Georgia review*. — *Vol. 37 (summer 1983) ; p. 392-409.*

AP2 .G375

Bibliographic footnotes.
The novel's focus is on selfhood—the mental processes engaged as a solitary man struggles against the united forces of international oppression. Selfhood is the last, most elusive enemy of totalitarianism. Newspeak is a mechanism for precluding the development of self concept.

Fink, Howard.
Newspeak : the epitome of parody techniques in *Nineteen Eighty-Four*. — In *Criti-*

cal survey. — Vol. 5 (summer 1971) ; p. 155-163.

Bibliographic footnotes.
Newspeak is a parody of an artificial language called Basic English that was popular in the thirties and forties. Orwell originally advocated its use but later saw its problems.

PN2 .C7

[George Orwell and 1984]. — **In** Revista de Occidente. — Nos. 33-34 (Feb./Mar. 1984) ; p. 7-223.

AP60 .R43

Several articles were translated for this special edition.
Contents: Presentación — Razón de estado y razón utópica / Ignacio Sotelo — Utopía y libertad / José Luis L. Aranguren — Utopía y esperanza cristiana / Manuel Fraijó Nieto — La Creación de la utopía en el cine / Antonio Lara — "1984" : Orwell y nosotros / Alain Besançon — Utopía y antiutopía : William Morris y George Orwell / Peter Stansky — Del diagnóstico a la pesadilla : Koestler, Orwell y el espíritu totalitario / John Wain — Las proyecciones de Orwell / Raymond Williams — Orwell y la guerra civil española / Raymond Carr — De la utopía al totalitarismo / Fernando Claudín — Sociología del totalitarismo / Luciano Pellicani — "1984" : sociopatología de la conciencia fiscal / Fernando Savater — El Desafío libertario, notas sobre Nozick / Bill Puka — Los Fundamentos económicos de la libertad / Francisco Cabrillo.

Harris, Harold J.
Orwell's essays and 1984. — **In** Twentieth century literature. — Vol. 4 (Jan. 1959) ; p. 154-161.

PN2 .T8

Howe, Irving.
"1984"—Utopia reversed. — **In** New International. — Vol. 16 (Nov./Dec. 1950) ; p. 360-368.

HX1 .N35

Hynes, Samuel Lynn.
Twentieth century interpretations of 1984 : a collection of critical essays / edited by Samuel Hynes. — Englewood Cliffs, N.J. : Prentice-Hall, [1971]. — vi, 117 p. — (Twentieth century interpretations) (A spectrum book)

PR6029.R8 N55

Contents: Introduction / Samuel Hynes — PART ONE REVIEWS: 1984 / V. S. Pritchett ; Orwell on the future / Lionel Trilling — PART TWO ESSAYS: 1984, the mysticism of cruelty / Isaac Deutscher ; 1984, history as nightmare / Irving Howe ; The strangled cry / John Strachey ; Introduction to 1984 / Stephen Spender ; The road to 1984 / George Kateb ; Orwell and the techniques of didactic fantasy / Alex Zwerdling — PART THREE VIEWPOINTS: Letter to George Orwell / Aldous Huxley ; 1984 / Herbert Read ; Climax and change / Wyndham Lewis ; From The English Utopia / A. L. Morton — Chronology of important dates. — Notes on the editor and contributors — Selected bibliography.

Lewis, Peter.
George Orwell, the road to 1984 / Peter Lewis. — 1st American ed. — New York : Harcourt Brace Jovanovich, c1981. — 122 p. : ill., ports.

R6029.R8 Z726 1981

Bibliography: p. 117.

Lyons, John O.
George Orwell's opaque glass in *1984*. — In *Wisconsin studies in contemporary literature.* — *Vol. 2 (fall 1961) ; p. 39-46.*
PN2 .W55
Points out recurring references to eye glasses and dirty windows.

Maddison, Michael.
1984 : a Burnhamite fantasy. — In *Political quarterly.* — *Vol. 32 (Jan./Mar. 1961) ; p. 71-79.*
JA8 .P72
James Burnham in *The Managerial Revolution* suggested the three superstates and emphasized class struggle.

Meyers, Jeffrey.
The evolution of "1984." — In *English miscellany.* — *Vol. 23 (1972) ; p. 247-261.*
PR13 .E45
Bibliographic footnotes.
The work is "a fantasy in the form of a naturalistic novel." Its material is from the present and the past and its themes and symbols can be identified in Orwell's earlier works.

***Nineteen Eighty-Four* to 1984** : a companion to the classic novel of our times / edited by C. J. Kuppig. — New York : Caroll & Graf, 1984. — 316 p.
PR6029.R8 N5325 1984
Includes bibliographical references.
"Chronology of Important Dates" / Samuel L. Hynes: p. 311-312.
Collected essays, comments and reviews all of which have been published elsewhere.

On *Nineteen eighty-four* / edited by Peter Stansky. — Stanford, Calif. : Stanford Alumni Association, c1983. — 228 p. : ill. — (The Portable Stanford)
PR6029.R8 N644 1983b
Includes bibliographical references.
Also published in New York by W. H. Freeman in 1983.
Contents: I. THE BOOK, THE MAN, THE YEAR: *Nineteen Eighty-Four*, the book / William Abrahams ; Orwell, the man / Peter Stansky ; 1939 and 1984, George Orwell and the vision of judgement / Alex Comfort — II. WAR IS PEACE: Triangularity and international violence / Gordon A. Craig ; Newspeak and Nukespeak / Sidney D. Drell ; The Economics of *Nineteen Eighty-Four* / Kenneth J. Arrow ; 1984, population and environment / Paul R. Ehrlich and Anne H. Ehrlich ; Economic doublethink, food and politics / Scott R. Pearson ; The Politics of technology and the technology of politics / Robert E. McGinn ; The Biomedical revolution and totalitarianism control / Raymond B. Clayton — III. IGNORANCE IS STRENGTH: Lawspeak and doublethink / Barbara Allen Babcock ; Newspeak, could it really work / Elizabeth Closs Traugott ; Winston Smith, the last humanist / Ian Watt ; "You're only a rebel from the waist downwards," Orwell's view of women / Anne K. Mellor ; Television and telescreen / Martin Esslin ; Smokey Bear as Big Brother / Marion Levenstein — IV. FREEDOM IS SLAVERY: For the love of Big Brother, the sexual politics of *Nineteen Eighty-Four* / Paul Robinson ; Zamyatin's *We* and *Nineteen Eighty-Four* / Edward J. Brown ; The proles of Airstrip One / Gerald Dorfman ; Totalterror / Robert Conquest ; Big Brother is watching you / Alexander Dallin ; Mind control, political fiction and psychological reality / Philip G. Zimbardo — Reader's guide.

Orwell issue : *1984*. — In *College literature.* — *Vol. 11 (no. 1, 1984) ; p. 1-94.*
PR1 .C65

Developed in conjunction with a symposium held at West Chester University, West Chester, Pa., in October 1983.
Contents: *1984* : Oceania as an ideal state / Gorman Beauchamp — Orwell's "Second Thoughts on James Burnham" and 1984 / R. B. Reaves — The Death of Big Sister : Orwell's tragic message / Joan Weatherly — Orwell in 1984 / John Atkins — Orwell on religion : the Catholic and Jewish questions / John Rodden — Orwell's language of waste land and trench / Claire Hopley — Sources and non-sources : "Politics and the English Language" / W. F. Bolton — Ideology and personality in Orwell's criticism / Graham Good — Trends in Orwell criticism / Paul Schlueter.

Patai, Daphne.
Gamesmanship and androcentrism in Orwell's *1984* — In *Modern Language Association of America. PMLA. Publications of the Modern Language Association.* — *Vol. 97 (Oct. 1982)* ; p. 856–870.

PB6 .M6

The conflict of the novel is in the struggle of two men, victim and tormentor, who share the same reference frames and fundamental values. "Examining these values leads to a critique of Orwell's androcentrism and misogny."

Plank, Robert.
George Orwell's guide through hell : a psychological study of 1984 / by Robert Plank. — San Bernardino, Calif. : Borgo Press, 1984. — [96 p.]. — (The Milford series. Popular writers of today, 0163-2469 ; vol. 41)
Not yet in LC collection.

Rahv, Philip.
The unfuture of Utopia. — In *Partisan review.* — *Vol. 16 (July 1949)* ; p. 743–749.

HX1 .P3

Reilly, Patrick.
Nineteen Eighty-Four : the failure of humanism. — In *Critical quarterly.* — *Vol. 24 (autumn 1982)* ; p. 19–30.

AP4 .C887

Winston Smith is all of humanity, with the defects and faults that outweigh humanist hopes and yearnings for nobility.

Roazen, Paul.
Orwell, Freud and *1984*. — In *Virginia quarterly review.* — *Vol. 54 (autumn 1978)* ; p. 675–695.

AP2 .V76

Notes parallel aspects of their writing without suggesting that there was influence. However, *Nineteen Eighty-Four* does have "a Freudian air."

Slater, Joseph.
The fictional values of *1984*. — In *Kirk, Rudolf. — Essays in literary history : presented to J. Milton French / edited by Rudolf Kirk and C. F. Main. — New York : Russell & Russell, 1965.* — p. 249–264.

PR14 .K5

Small, Christopher.
The road to Miniluv : George Orwell, the state, and God / by Christopher Small. — [Pittsburgh] : University of Pittsburgh Press, 1976, c1975. — 220 p.

PR6029.R8 Z786 1976

Bibliography: p. [9]-10.

Smith, Marcus.
The wall of blackness : a psychological approach to *1984*. — **In** *Modern fiction studies*. — *Vol. 14 (winter 1968-69)* ; *p. 423-433*.
PS379 .M55

Bibliographic footnotes.
Winston is an Oedipal figure in search of a substitute mother.

Smyer, Richard I.
1984 : the search for the golden country. — **In** *Arizona quarterly*. — *Vol. 27 (spring 1971)* ; *p. 41-52*.
AP2 .A7265

Bibliographic footnotes.
Offers a psychoanalytic interpretation showing how the novel represents an inner condition fraught with anxiety and primitive tensions.

Sperber, Murray.
"Gazing into the glass paperweight" : the structure and psychology of Orwell's *1984*. — **In** *Modern fiction studies*. — *Vol. 26 (summer 1980)* ; *p. 213-226*.
PS379 .M55

Finds roots of *Nineteen Eighty-Four* in Orwell's accounts of his boyhood—his puritanical English home and boarding school—and in his understanding of paranoid fantasies.

Steinhoff, William R.
George Orwell and the origins of *1984* / William Steinhoff. — Ann Arbor : University of Michigan Press, [1975]. — 288 p.
PR6029.R8 N67

Bibliography: p. 253-268.
Published with the title *The Road to 1984* in London by Weidenfeld and Nicolson in 1975 (PR6029.R8 Z794).

Steinhoff, William R.
Utopia reconsidered : comments on *1984* / William Steinhoff. — **In** *No place else : explorations in utopian and dystopian fiction* / edited by Eric S. Rabkin, Martin H. Greenberg, Joseph D. Olander. — Carbondale : Southern Illinois University Press, c1983. — *p. 147-161*.
PR830.U7 N6 1983

Bibliographical references included in "Notes" (p. 160-161).

Wilt, Judith.
Behind the door of *1984* : "the worst thing in the world." **In** *Modernism reconsidered* / edited by Robert Kiely, assisted by John Hildebidle. — Cambridge, Mass. : Harvard University Press, 1983. — *p. 247-262*.
PR478.M6 M62 1983

Bibliographic footnotes.
Explores the importance of the rat as the ultimate symbol of horror and terror for Winston Smith, George Orwell, and others.

Yorks, Samuel A.
George Orwell : seer over his shoulder. — **In** *Bucknell review*. — *Vol. 9 (Mar. 1960)* ; *p. 32-45*.
AP2 .B887

Suggests that the school day tyranny and discipline that Orwell experienced in his youth contributed to his ability to imagine torment under totalitarianism.

Comparison with Other Works

Beauchamp, Gorman.
Of man's last disobedience : Zamiatin's *We* and Orwell's *1984*. — In *Comparative literature studies.* — Vol. 10 (Dec. 1973) ; p. 285-301.

Bibliographic references included in "Notes" (p. 298-301).
        PN851 .C63
In both works the individual's rebellion against the state parallels the Christian myth of Adam's disobedience against God.

Brown, Edward James.
Brave New World, 1984*, and *We : an essay on Anti-Utopia : (Zamyatin and English literature) / E. J. Brown. — Ann Arbor : Ardis, c1976. — 61 p. : ill. — (Ardis essay series ; no. 4)

Bibliography: p. 57-61.
        PG3476.Z34 M933

Browning, Gordon.
Toward a set of standards for [evaluating] anti-Utopian fiction. — In *Cithara.* — Vol. 10 (Dec. 1970) ; p. 18-32.

Bibliographic footnotes.
        AS36 .S2
Discussion of *We*, *Nineteen Eighty-Four*, and *Brave New World*.

Calder, Jenni.
Huxley and Orwell, Brave New World and Nineteen Eighty Four / by Jenni Calder. — London : Edward Arnold, 1976. — 61 p. — (Studies in English literature ; no. 63)

Bibliography: p. [60].
        PR6015.U9 B6727

Geering, R. G.
***Darkness at Noon* and *1984*—a comparative study.** — In *Australian quarterly.* — Vol. 30 (Sept. 1958) ; p. 90-96.

        DU80 .A95

Hamilton, Kenneth M.
G. K. Chesterton and George Orwell : a contrast in prophecy. — In *Dalhousie review.* — Vol. 31 (autumn 1951) ; p. 198-205.

        AP5 .D3

Jones, Joseph.
Utopia as dirge. — In *American quarterly.* — Vol. 2 (fall 1950) ; p. 214-226.
        AP2 .A3985
Considers the disquieting notion of mourning for the future while comparing *Nineteen Eighty-Four*, *Brave New World*, and *A Connecticut Yankee in King Arthur's Court*.

Kessler, Martin.
Power and the perfect state : a study in disillusionment as reflected in Orwell's *Nineteen Eighty-Four* and Huxley's *Brave New World*. — In *Political science quarterly.* — Vol. 72 (Dec. 1957) ; p. 565-577.

        H1 .P8

Patai, Daphne.
Orwell's despair, Burdekin's hope : gender and power in dystopia. — In *Women's studies international forum.* — Vol. 7 (no. 2, 1984) ; p. 85-95.
HQ1101 .W776

Comparison of *Nineteen Eighty-Four* and Katharine Burdekin's futuristic novel, *Swastika Night,* in which women have been systematically oppressed into ignorant and fearful animals useful only for breeding.

Siegel, Paul N.
The cold war : *1984* twenty-five years later. — In *Confrontation.* — Vol. 8 (spring 1974) ; p. 148-156.
PS501 .C66

Explores the effect of James Burnham's *The Managerial Revolution* on Orwell's writing.

Spender, Stephen.
Anti-vision and despair. — In his *The creative element : a study of vision, despair and orthodoxy among some modern writers.* — Freeport, N.Y. : Books for Libraries Press, [1971, c1953]. — p. 125-139.
PN771 .S63 1971

Observations on *Nineteen Eighty-Four* and T. S. Eliot's *The Waste Land.*

Stansky, Peter.
Utopia and antiutopia : William Morris and George Orwell. — In *History today.* — Vol. 33 (Feb. 1983) ; p. 33-38 : ill.
D1 .H818

First published in *The Threepenny Review,* summer 1982.
Compares *Nineteen Eighty-Four* and Morris's optimistic utopian work, *News from Nowhere,* published in 1890.

Struc, Roman S.
George Orwell's *Nineteen Eighty-Four* and Dostoevsky's "Underground Men." — In *Pacific Northwest Conference on Foreign Languages. Proceedings.* — Vol. 24 (1973). — Corvallis, Ore. : The Conference, 1973. — p. 217-220.
PB11 .P2

NINETEEN EIGHTY-FOUR TODAY

A CBS television news special addressed the question Has Orwell's world come or is it coming? Entitled "1984 Revisited," the program was broadcast in June of 1983 with Walter Cronkite as the anchorman. A copy of the telecast is in the custody of the Library's Motion Picture and Television Reading Room.

Allen, Francis A.
***Nineteen Eighty-Four* and the eclipse of private worlds.** — In *Michigan quarterly review.* — Vol. 22 (fall 1983) ; p. 517-540.
AS30 .M48

Today the state is engaged in a "comprehensive assault on the private world of its subjects." With destruction of the past and its record, the individual becomes dependent on the state for memory. Assaults on individual privacy continue to be noted in contemporary society and should be carefully watched.

Burgess, Anthony.
1985 / Anthony Burgess. — 1st ed. — Boston : Little, Brown, c1978. — 272 p.
PZ4 .B953Ni [PR6052 .U638]
Contents: Part I, 1984 — Part II, 1985 — Epilogue.
The first part contains several essays analyzing various aspects of Orwell's work and thought. The second is an alternative novel set in the future. The epilogue offers additional considerations about past and future. "In an idyllic 1984, the 1984 of Orwell's vision will still serve as a symbol of humanity's worst fears."

Burris, Keith.
The defense of private decency : More on Orwell, his vision and his limits. — In *Commonweal*. — Vol. 110 (May 20, 1983) ; p. 299-301.
AP2 .C6897
The modern world tends to concentrate power and does so at the expense of privacy.

Cornish, Edward.
An Inquiry into George Orwell's *1984* / [special section compiled by] Edward Cornish. — In *Futurist*. — Vol. 12 (Dec. 1983) ; p. 21-32, 49-51, 53-59.
CB158 .F88
Contents: George Orwell's *1984* / Burnham P. Beckwith — *1984*, the year that never came / W. Warren Wagar — As April's green endures : hope in Orwell's *1984* / John V. Knapp — Breakfast at Big Brother's / Ralph E. Hamil — A chronology for *1984* / Ralph E. Hamil — The enduring nightmare : the *1984* bureaucracy / Gary Gappert — Beyond Orwell : the need for new myths / Robert Theobald — Contradictory visions : American optimism vs. Orwell's *1984* / Thomas L. Trumble and Ursula Meese.

Doctorow, E. L.
On the brink of 1984. — In *Playboy*. — Vol. 30 (Feb. 1983) ; p. 78-80, 156-158, 160, 162.
AP2 .P692 Rare Bk Coll
When governments act without thought of responsibility to their people, when "clubbing history dumb and rendering language insensible" are regular practices, and nuclear stockpiling is accompanied by intermittent little wars, then Orwell's prophecy does not seem far off the mark.

Fagan, C.
Fighting for 1984. — In *Canadian forum*. — Vol. 63 (Dec. 1983) ; p. 39-41.
AP5 .C125
Notes that American writers are hurrying to write about Orwell and speculating on how he would have viewed America.

Feagler, Dick.
1984, its finally here. — In *Cleveland magazine*. — Vol. 13 (Jan. 1984) ; p. 72-75, 112.

F499.C6 C57

The Future of Nineteen Eighty-Four / edited and with an introduction by Ejner J. Jensen. — Ann Arbor : University of Michigan Press, c1984. — viii, 209 p.
PR6029.R8 N533 1984
Contents: *Nineteen Eighty-Four*, satire or prophecy? / Bernard Crick — George Orwell and the English language / Richard W. Bailey — "I'm not literary, dear" / Leslie

Tentler — From bingo to Big Brother / Gorman Beauchamp — Orwell's psychopolitics / Alex Zwerdling — The Self and memory in *Nineteen Eighty-Four* / Joseph Adelson — The Political theory of pessimism / Alfred G. Meyer — George Orwell / Eugene J. McCarthy — *Nineteen Eighty-Four* and the eclipse of private worlds / Francis A. Allen — George Orwell as political secretary of the Zeitgeist / W. Warren Wagar — Afterword / William R. Steinhoff.

Goodman, David.
Countdown to 1984 : Big Brother may be right on schedule. — In *Futurist*. — Vol. 12 (Dec. 1978) ; p. 345-348, 350-352, 355 : ill.
CB158 .F88
Includes a list of scientific and technological predictions derived from Orwell's novel that "have either come true or could soon come true."
Responses from readers were published in the issues of Vol. 13 for April 1979 (p. 110-117) and August 1979 (p. 291-293, 295-296).

Gottlieb, Annie.
Is "1984" really here? — In *McCall's*. — Vol. III (Jan. 1984) ; p. 20, 96, 98-101, 119.
TT500 .M2
Collection of comments from prominent men and women comparing Orwell's 1984 with circumstances today. Commentators include Walter Mondale, Gloria Steinem, John Glenn, Norman Lear, Jesse Jackson, John Naisbitt, Phyllis Schlafly, Helen Caldicott, Carl Bernstein, and Arthur Schlesinger, Jr., who notes that Orwell's novel belongs not to the literature of prophecy, "but to the literature of warning."

Gray, Paul.
That year is almost here / by Paul Gray ; reported by Anne Hopkins, New York and John Saar, London. — In *Time*. — Vol. 122 (Nov. 28, 1983) ; p. 46-48, 53-54, 56 : ill.
AP2 .T37
Reviews the outpouring of comment on *Nineteen Eighty-Four*, notes several examples, and summarizes Orwell's life and work.

Grenier, Richard.
Comment [on *1984*]. — In *Chronicles of Culture*. — Vol. 8 (Jan. 1984) ; p. 4-5, 38.
PN80 .C57
Orwell warned of the "horrors of totalitarianism particularly of the Soviet variety." However, he overestimated the ability of the state to obliterate memory and never guessed that doublethink could thrive in a democratic society.

Harrington, Michael.
***Nineteen Eighty-Four* revisited**. — In *Orwell, George*. — *Orwell's Nineteen eighty-four : text, sources, criticism* / edited by Irving Howe. — 2nd ed. — New York : Harcourt Brace Jovanovich, c1982. — p. 429-439.
PR6029.R8 N647 1982
English socialism has not become totalitarianism. However, the trend toward collectivization is a critical trend of the 1980s throughout the world.

Is this 1984? : essays from the perspective of the humanities / edited by Virgil Grillo, Marilynn Sawin. — [Denver] : University of Colorado, c1984. — vi, 159 leaves.
PR6029.R8 N535 1984

Includes bibliographies.

Jensen, Ejner J.
1984 : the language and ideas of Orwell's book have fixed themselves in our awareness. — In *Horizon (New York).* — Vol. 27 (Jan./Feb. 1984) ; p. 14-15.
AP2 .H788

Johnson, Paul.
Orwellian overkill. — In *Spectator.* — Vol. 252 (Jan. 7 1984) ; p. 13-14.
AP4 .S7
Talk about Orwell and his predictions has exceeded reasonable limits. He has been "turned upside down and stood on his short-back-and-sides head."

Jones, George E.
"1984" how close to reality? — In *U.S. news and world report.* — Vol. 86 (Feb. 5, 1979) ; p. 49-50 : ill.
JK1 .U65
On the whole, America today seems far from *Nineteen Eighty-Four*, but there are similarities which demonstrate the need for watchfulness and moral wisdom in planning for tomorrow.

Kagan, Daniel.
Big Brother is closing in. — In *Penthouse.* — Vol. 15 (Jan. 1984) ; p. 60-62, 156, 158-159.

AP2 .P413 Rare Bk Coll

Labedz, Leopold.
Can Orwell survive 1984? : of doublethink & double-talk, body-snatching & other silly pranks. — In *Encounter (London).* — Vol. 63 (June-July/Aug. 1984) ; p. 11-24 ; 25-34 : ill.
AP4 .E44
Extensive analysis of current studies and commentary on Orwell and his work. "More often than not he has been misunderstood and generally trivialized and his insights wilfully distorted."

McCormick, Donald.
Approaching 1984 / Donald McCormick. — Newton Abbot [Eng.] : David & Charles, c1980. — 191 p.

Bibliography: p. 187.
PR6029.R8 N64
Similarities between modern society and Orwell's world include sex without love, unending war, linguistic manipulation, doublethink, and computerized control of behavior.

Malkin, Lawrence.
Halfway to 1984. — In *Horizon.* — Vol. 12 (spring 1970) ; p. 33-39 : ill.
AP2 .H788
Orwell may have underestimated the "strength of European culture in resisting the encroachments of the machine age."

Messerer, Azary.
Orwell and the Soviet Union. — In *etc. : a review of general semantics.* — Vol. 41 (summer 1984) ; p. 130-134.

B840 .E85

The entire issue is devoted to a general analysis of the present and future, based rather loosely on Orwell's *Nineteen Eighty-Four*.

Next year is nineteen eighty-four. — In *Impact of science on society.* — (no. 2, 1983) ; p. 149-158.

Q1 .I4

Entire issue devoted to Orwell and his novel.
Contents: Comment / Robert H. Maybury — Nineteen Eighty-Four : from fiction to reality / Armelle Gauffenic — An Evolving man-machine relationship / Bernard Dixon — Orwell's vision : the world in 1984 / Rahat Nabi Khan — The Control approach to dynamic behaviour / Emir A. Humo — The Computer in industry / Didier Leroux — Man and machine, an interactive and interadaptive system / Liu Haibo — Science and technology for a global society / Denis Goulet — 1984 : the impact of science on society / Hermann Bondi and J. M. Bates — On the proper application of the human sciences : love making as a political act / Pierre-Philippe Druet — Individuality and pluralistic images of the nature of man / Joyce R. Royce and Arnold Powell.

Nineteen eighty-four in 1984 : autonomy, control, and communication / edited by Paul Chilton and Crispin Aubrey. — London : Comedia Pub. Group ; London ; New York : Marion Boyars, 1983. — 120 p., [3] leaves of plates. — (Comedia series ; no. 17)

PR6029.R8 N643

Contents: Introduction — INTERPRETATIONS: The Making of 1984 / Crispin Aubrey ; Reclaiming Orwell / David Widgery ; Desire is thoughtcrime / Jenny Taylor — COMMUNICATIONS: Newspeak, it's the real thing / Paul Chilton ; The Tyranny of language / Florence Lewis and Peter Moss — TECHNOLOGIES: Taming the universal machine / Christopher Roper ; The Robots's return? / Mike Cooley and Mike Johnson ; Information as power / Paul Lashmar — Environment: Big Brother drives a bulldozer / Colin Ward ; Hard machines, soft messages / Philip Corrigan ; The Conscription of history / Patrick Wright — Biographies — Notes.

1984 : the dawn or dusk of a terrifying concept. — In *Loyola magazine.* — Vol. 13 (fall 1984) ; p. 6-9.
Not identified in LC collection.
Commentary from a two day symposium "George Orwell : Images of the Twentieth Century" held at Loyola University. Concerns voiced included creeping newspeak and the pervasive presence of the media.

1984 revisited : totalitarianism in our century / edited by Irving Howe. — 1st ed. — New York : Harper & Row, c1983. — x, 276 p.

PR6029.R8 N5 1983

Contents: 1984 : enigmas of power / Irving Howe — The Fate of *1984* / Mark Crispin Miller — "The Golden country" : sex and love in *1984* / Elaine Hoffman Baruch — Orwell and the English language / Bernard Avishai — *1984* on Staten Island / Luther P. Carpenter — Does Big Brother really exist? / Robert C. Tucker — On "failed totalitarianism" / Michael Walzer — Totalitarianism and the virtue of the lie / Leszek Kolakowski — The Disintegration of Leninist totalitarianism / Milovan Djilas — *1984* : decade of the experts? / Johanno Strasser — *1984*, the ingredients of totalitarianism / James B. Rule — *1984* and the conservative imagination / Robert Nisbet — Beyond totalitarianism / Richard Lowenthal.

Orwells Jahr : ist die Zukunft von gestern die Gegenwart von heute? / Dieter Hasselblatt (Hrsg.). — Frankfurt/Main : Ullstein, c1983. — 279 p. : ill.

PR6029.R8 N4936 1983

Orwell's "1984"—coming true? — In *U.S. news & world report.* — *Vol. 95 (Dec. 26, 1983/Jan. 2, 1984) ; p. 86-91, 93-95. : ill. (part col.)*

JK1 .U6

Contents: Orwell's "1984"—coming true? / Abigail Trafford — Big Brother's tools are ready, but . . . / Stanley N. Wellborn — U.S. still a far cry from world of "1984" / Susanna McBee — For a peek at "1984," look to East Germany / Stewart Powell — Language takes a turn for "plusungood" / David A. Wiessler.

Orwell's world : how close? — In *World Press review.* — *Vol. 30 (Dec. 1983) ; p. 33-40 : ill.*

AP2 .A833

Contents: Vision and reality : dictatorship, doublethink, and dehumanization / Mario Pontes ; excerpted from Jornal do Brasil — Controlling technology : toward a balance of freedom and progress / Janet Morgan ; Sunday Times magazine — An Orwellian world? The view from nine foreign editors' desks.

Podhoretz, Norman.
If Orwell were alive today. — In *Harper's.* — *Vol. 266 (Jan. 1983) ; p. 30-32, 34-37 : ill.*

AP2 .H3

Speculates that Orwell would have rejected his socialist position and come to align himself with the neoconservatives who are warning against Soviet imperialism and calling for a strong defense posture. A response by Christopher Hitchens and reply by Podhoretz appear in the February issue (p. 56-58).

Stafford, Tim.
1984 : can Orwell's nightmare still become reality? — In *Christianity today.* — *Vol. 28 (Jan. 13, 1984) ; p. 22-26.*

BR1 .C6418

The novel deals with the struggle between good and evil and Orwell assumes that evil will win. But love can outlast selfishness; Christian faith can give an individual strength to survive oppression.

Steiner, George.
Killing time. — In *New Yorker.* — *Vol. 59 (Dec. 12, 1983) ; p. 168, 171, 172-178, 181-182, 184, 186, 188.*

AP2 .N6763

There is no comparable case in which an author has staked his claim in advance to a particular piece of time. Blackened before its arrival this year has been denied a place in "the calendar of hope." The act of putting one's signature on a year represents a tremendous imposition of one man's imagination on generations of readers.

Syrkin, Marie.
Orwell's "protective stupidity" in 1984. — In *Midstream; a monthly Jewish review.* — *Vol. 30 (Jan. 1984) ; p. 37-39.*

DS149 .A336

Questions why "true believers" on any side of an issue seem to blind themselves to criticism of their views, even in a society where there is freedom to question.

Threshold of apocalypse : 1984 and after. — In *World literature today.* — *Vol. 58 (spring 1984) ; p. 189-208.*

Z1007 .B717

Contents: Writing against Big Brother : notes on apocalyptic fiction in South Africa / Andre Brink — A Vision of the apocalypse / Elie Wiesel ; translated from the French by Joan Grimbert and the author — What Orwell did not foresee / Gunter Kunert ; translated from the German by William Riggan — *Nineteen Eighty-Four* in Germany : a look back / Sidney Rosenfeld — Versions of doublethink in *Gravity's Rainbow*, *Darkness Visible*, *Ridley Walker* and *Travels to the Enu* / Roy Arthur Swanson.

Wain, John.
Dear George Orwell. — In *American scholar.* — Vol. 52 (winter 1982) ; p. 21-37.
AP2 .A4572
Orwell was substantially correct about the continuing behavior of the Communist Party and the essential nature of communism, but he did not forecast a rise of Big Labor and trade unions so powerful that they could make demands "far in excess of a fair day's pay for a fair day's work."

Wagschal, Peter H.
1984—a second look. — In *World futures.* — Vol. 18 (no. 3/4, 1982) ; p. 285-290.
B1 .P25
Techniques of "Newspeak" and doublethink" as exemplified in American advertising practices contribute to the special control of behavior. Thought control and the rewriting of history, while not as blatantly practiced as in Orwell's novel, appear regularly in America.